From Crawley to Carlisle

From Crawley to Carlisle
A Trawl around League Two

Chris Upfield

Matador
9 Priory Business Park,
Wistow Road, Kibworth Beauchamp,
Leicestershire. LE8 0RX
Tel: 0116 279 2299
Email: books@troubador.co.uk
Web: www.troubador.co.uk/matador
Twitter: @matadorbooks

ISBN 978 1785898 785

British Library Cataloguing in Publication Data.
A catalogue record for this book is available from the British Library.

Printed and bound by CPI Group (UK) Ltd, Croydon, CR0 4YY
Typeset in 11pt Aldine401 BT by Troubador Publishing Ltd, Leicester, UK

Matador is an imprint of Troubador Publishing Ltd

CHAPTER 1

CAMBRIDGE

"It was rubbish, really rubbish" the middle aged Cambridge supporter spat into his 'phone. I marvelled how he could get the words out as he only had a solitary tooth and even that balanced precariously downwards from his top gum like a slowly melting stalactite. Still, at least he was probably not far from home and would soon be in front of a warm fire. I ventured a guess that as he walked out of our earshot his next words to the wife would be "I've had me two pints in the social club, I'll be home in 10 minutes and I'm hungry. If dinner's not on the table, I'm kicking seven shades out of the cat". He was entitled to be upset. His team had just been beaten 6-2 at home by the team with the worst away record in the league. Namely, Pompey, the team I'd supported for 50 years

I was by now frozen to the bone, and bored. It was nearly 6pm and we'd been waiting for nearly an hour for our taxi to arrive to take us back to our hotel. I guessed that Panther taxis of Cambridge had recently been bought out by South-west Trains, who had imposed their own service standards upon their new subsidiary. In truth that is probably unfair. Panther taxis are probably a very good transport company but working within the confines of a Cambridge road and traffic flow system which had been thought through by a man with shares

1

in "Gridlock Creation UK Ltd", their timekeeping stats didn't stand a chance.

Thinking of the man with one tooth, my boredom extended to going through the alphabet to identify which letters it was impossible to pronounce without any teeth. I worked out that F,L, S,T,V and Z fall pretty squarely into that category and sh and th were nearly impossible, especially at the start of a word. I realised why the man with the tooth hadn't said that his team was "totally shit" or "very substandard". I surmised that he would have trouble telling people that he had a stutter. My hysteria took me to even greater lengths. I wondered how a toothless Spaniard ever got served beer, or how a gummy German interrogator ever convinced any POW that they had ways of making them talk. Eventually, these inane thoughts passed and I reviewed in my own mind how we got to be standing like ice statues outside the Abbey Stadium.

Our weekend in Cambridge had been planned for some time, in fact from the day Premier Inn launched their £29 a night promotion. My daughter Nicola had been set to work to find us a weekend away where we could have a night in an attractive city whilst taking in a Pompey away game, and she came up with Cambridge in February. Having procured the hotel at modest cost we splashed out on a hospitality package.

Friends were corralled into joining us for the weekend and ultimately we mustered 4 couples as well as diverse adult children including two of mine, Nicola and Paddy. I'd stayed in Cambridge a couple of years before with my wife Michelle whilst taking in a weekend's racing at nearby Newmarket, so had enjoyed the delights of central Cambridge, and we decided that we'd drive up on the Saturday morning; our friends Andy, Bev, Steve, Sue, Chopper (Cliff as opposed to Ron) and Toni wanted a bit longer to experience the sights, so had gone up the night before.

We arrived at the Premier Inn on the outskirts of

Cambridge at about 10.45. Michelle and I had devoured crumpets for breakfast, but the kids had passed, preferring an extra 15 minutes in bed. As we'd booked into a hospitality package at the ground with Andy and Bev, I reckoned that crumpets would be enough to see me through to lunchtime. It's one of my bugbears that everything with my kids (boys in particular) is Lastminute.com and they seem to have no idea of preparation or planning. So on arrival at the hotel at the fag end of breakfast, and notwithstanding that they would be sitting down to what we hoped would be a sumptuous 3-course banquet in less than two hours, Paddy decided that he needed "something to keep me going" which in his case consisted of a dozen rashers of bacon, eight sausages, three eggs and the equivalent of a tin of beans. Ok, I exaggerate but it was certainly enough that I couldn't see how he could possibly find space for lunch. Even Nicola with a less voracious appetite tucked away enough to make me question whether the money spent on procuring a hospitality package was to be wasted.

The hospitality idea had been Andy's. He'd figured that our fixtures after Christmas were such that by the time this game came around, we might be on a long-awaited run of wins. With Cambridge just two hours away from Portsmouth and knowing how little it takes for a Pompey fan's mood to change from despair to unjustified optimism, he was worried we might book the hotel and then find we couldn't get this number of tickets. He had previously been in charge of the rail network on the Isle of Wight (which actually consists of just one line from Ryde to Sandown) and learned that some of his ex-workmates had booked hospitality to guarantee entry. We decided to do the same. I struck a deal with the kids that they would pay the basic ticket price and I'd top up for the hospitality element. It has to be remembered that this is League 2 hospitality; we had long ago forsaken the dizzy heights of the Premier League where a day in a hospitality box even for a game against the likes of Stoke would set you back the cost of an all-inclusive week in Lloret de Mar. I think it worked out at £60 a head including the match ticket.

We met up at the hotel with Steve, Sue, Andy and Bev and ordered a Panther 8-seater into town. We dropped off the hoi palloi who weren't going Corporate at a local hostelry and proceeded to the ground.

Our hospitality tickets had not arrived by the time we'd travelled and Andy went off to the ticket office to pick them up. After about 15 minutes when he failed to return we started to get concerned, but eventually he emerged triumphantly with an expression one might find on the face of someone who had just got World Cup final tickets knocked down on ebay. A tortuous set of alleyways took us round to the hospitality entrance where we were met by a female steward who obviously had the regular job of hospitality meet and greet. Not quite like Paul Scholes at Man United or Matt le Tissier at Southampton, more like one of the meeters and greeters at B and Q . She was wearing one of those yellow steward's jackets which would make Kate Moss look chunky, and she clearly took her job seriously. Carefully examining and tearing each ticket she'd hand each one back with the same words "enjoy the game" even though it was obvious that we were one party. It was like an automated supermarket checkout. I half expected her to hand back the last ticket and say "Please take your bag and your ticket. Thank you for shopping at Cambridge United".

We found our hospitality suite which proved to be a cut above a Portakabin if only because it had solid brick walls to three sides; the fourth was a sliding door which separated the toffs from the hand to mouth Cambridge fans drinking in the supporters club. There were about 12 tables crammed into a space not much bigger than a Regus office but you don't get your own private box for £60 and in fairness don't expect it.

We had been conveniently placed on a table with the railway boys from the Isle of Wight, presumably so friction was kept to a minimum.

It was past noon and the sun was over the yard-arm so the men felt reasonably justified in starting on the beer. The pre-match hospitality entertainment consisted of a football quiz sheet with 10 questions. We had a slight advantage over the local bigwigs in that one of the questions was "Who wears the Pompey no.12 shirt?" (The answer of course is the fans – isn't that the case even with Arbroath or Queen of the South? All football fans think they are the best and invariably their clubs indulge them in that thought) Andy and I taxed our brains to get seven of the answers and then passed the sheet to the isle of Wight boys who promptly consulted their 'phones, filled in the gaps and crossed out and replaced at least half of our answers.

The first course arrived – mushroom soup – it having taken about 45 minutes for the overburdened waitresses to get round the room with bread baskets, delicately placing what looked suspiciously like "bake in the oven" rolls on each side plate. By the time the soup arrived we had finished off the rolls in preference to resorting to cannibalism so the piece de resistance of Cambridge hospitality was unavailable to complement the starter. The soup had a tarmac sort of hue and in Michelle's opinion the use of mushroom had been somewhat spartan.

In contrast to the starter, the main course emerged quickly. A steak and stilton pie devoid of any hint of stilton, and minted peas lovingly poured from a tin. This was supplemented by a bowl of vegetables (probably of the Bird's Eye variety) which Robinson Crusoe would have considered ample but which was sadly inadequate for a table of eleven who resorted to separating the cauliflower florets and rationing the carrots just to add a flourish of colour to the plate. It was however perfectly sufficient for Nicola who covered up the fact that she was still stuffed from her late breakfast by protesting that she didn't much like pie. Paddy had polished off his plate before everyone else, clearly trying to establish that he has a square metre stomach capacity like a ruminant's innards. He even managed the passable lemon dessert.

Enter the Cambridge compere, who went by the name of Dave Doggett. Dave was obviously a passionate Cambridge United fan turned tireless worker (probably unpaid) for the club. He had a relaxed and genial air about him, though I couldn't help thinking that a name like Doggett in Portsmouth would invite jibes involving steamed up car windows on Portsdown Hill or Southsea seafront.

Dave's first job was to read out the quiz answers as a result of which we discovered that, aided by the Isle of Wight contingent's close study of Wikipedia, our table had won the bottle of wine offered as a prize. There were friendly (perhaps) boos from the Cambridge tables. Andy and I felt that accepting the prize would be like condoning Didier Drogba's best swallow dive. The Isle of Wight boys had no such scruples.

I glanced around the room and put the next table under greater scrutiny. One of their number was a throwback to the 1970s, who appeared to be acting as a host. I couldn't decide whether he looked most like the wrestler Jackie Pallo, Paul Nicholas or Alan Biley's brother. Alan Biley was I guessed a legend both at Cambridge and Pompey. He was best known at Portsmouth for a pre-Christmas game against Oxford when we were chasing promotion under Alan Ball. Trailing 1-0 at home the game extended into added time as a result of a pitch invasion by Santa Claus. In the last two minutes Biley notched two almost identical headers at the far post which turned defeat into victory. The moment was beautifully caught by a TV cameraman who had spotted manager Alan Ball's young son Jimmy nip out at 1-0 (presumably for a comfort break) returning just after our second goal hit the back of the net. Cue blubbing on the scale of a Gazza spitting image puppet, caught by the camera. Nowadays it would be a classic "third eye" on Soccer AM.

It transpired that as expected, the Paul Nicholas lookalike was indeed an ex-player for Cambridge in the John Beck glory days. I wondered if he'd been around in the time of Steve Claridge, also a dual Cambridge and Pompey legend.

Having presented the wine to the cheaters, Doggett Dave then introduced a Cambridge director, who gave the room an update as to how the extension to the hospitality suite was at planning application stage. The numbers he quoted for the cost could have been met by Wayne Rooney donating a couple of weeks' wages. Probably in fact no more than the cost of making the birthday cake that Yaya Toure didn't get. Such is the gulf between the Premier League and League Two. (I refuse to call it the .... Premier League. Isn't it irritating how every part of the media feels compelled to name the sponsor? Do they get some sort of kickback if they do?)

The director proceeded to read out the Cambridge team for the day. There were groans from the Cambridge supporters when the left back was named. When the Director shouted "Don't shoot the messenger" we realised that everyone thought he was crap and we were going to have some joy attacking down our right.

It was now time to take our seats which in the League Two caste system placed us just to the right of the half way line in slightly inferior seats to the Cambridge directors to our left. We were seated immediately in front of some Cambridge fans who'd probably paid top dollar, by League Two standards, for their tickets, certainly compared to their fellow fans slumped on the terraces opposite. The average age was such that, apart from one younger bloke sat on his own immediately behind us, it was a fair bet that a lot of heads would be bobbing down at half-time to extricate flasks of coffee from duffel bags.

The pitch was surveyed and found to be nothing like its glory days counterpart, when Cambridge were renowned for some under the belt tactics. It was said that their manager John Beck, who favoured route one football, forced the ground staff to leave the grass long in the corners so that long balls invariably resulted in Cambridge gaining ground. A bit like a rugby fly half not kicking for touch I suppose. Anyway this policy had obviously been abandoned because the pitch was in fine fettle. The away end was to our left, with a reasonably sizeable gap between the stand and the pitch which managed to soak up some of the noise which the away fans obviously thought they were making. The stand opposite us was for Cambridge seated fans, whilst to our right was a smallish covered terrace, which extended part way into the area of the ground opposite us. The ubiquitous home drummer was the centrepiece of this area.

Now at this stage you need to be aware exactly why we approached away games with a fatalistic defeatism. Apart from one early success we now had the worst away record in League Two. Cambridge were not pulling up trees but we surmised that they were probably going to be good enough to send most of our fans on yet another depressing journey home.

It was a pleasant surprise, therefore, that Pompey started briskly, and for once were clearly up for this one. Players were closed down quickly and tackles were committed. A turnover in the ruck after just two minutes released our star player Jed Wallace who cut in and sent a firm finish into the corner. The hospitality area erupted – well, about 10% of it anyway, probably less if you take into account that Michelle and Bev just clapped furtively. The sole under pensionable age non-coffee drinker immediately behind us was unimpressed and told us in blunt tone to go forth and multiply. I suppose I could understand why he'd be upset that his top price seat was on this day immediately behind a bunch of Pompey fans who'd infiltrated the hospitality. For a split second Paddy and

I were a little wary of his aggressive intentions but frankly he lost his street cred when he followed up with "He was offside anyway" On the basis that Jed had beaten at least two players in waltzing through their defence we just turned round and laughed.

We proceeded to dominate the next 15 minutes without scoring again. All was undone in typical Portsmouth fashion when our right back Joe Devera tried to keep in play a loose pass but only succeeded in doing the honours for the Cambridge left-winger who skipped away and buried a fine angled finish to make it 1-1. Mendez-Laing was the winger's name and we remembered him from a few unproductive games on loan for us a couple of seasons earlier. Comments had been made at that time that he had the fattest backside in the lower leagues which made his sudden turn of foot somewhat surprising. A new phrase had been coined about our strikers at the time – "Couldn't hit Mendez-Laing's arse with a banjo".

Joe Devera was clutching his head in shame and I expected the usual ironic chant of "Joe Devera football genius" to erupt from our fans but generally Joe was a committed and solid defender whilst being extremely uncomfortable on the ball. Hence the ironic but not malicious chant. But we generally don't like to get on our own players backs when they are seen to be giving all, and Joe escaped without hurtful banter.

Having dominated play we were now on level terms and feared the usual awayday blues. Gobshite behind us was getting cocky, but that lasted only a couple of minutes when our recent signing Matt Tubbs curled in a great shot after Jed had set him up. We started to cut through their defence like butter and won a corner which, after a partial clearance, our best defender Paul Robinson buried. The hospitality box was now getting embarrassing and Gobshite pissed off furtively for an early half–time cheeseburger, like Captain Oates never to be seen again.

At this point, Andy's bladder gave out on him, a not unknown occurrence, and he disappeared down the hospitality tunnel, re-emerging too late to see the best move of the game with on fire Jed again getting away down the left and crossing for Matt Tubbs to plant a header past the keeper. The knowledge that we were 4-1 up at half time meant that unlike little Jimmy Ball, Andy didn't blub at missing the goal.

The whistle blew and we went down for our half time tea and cheese and biscuits including the stilton that hadn't been discernible in the pie.

Now at this point, there were probably a good hundred fans who'd put on £50 at 9/4 for a Pompey away win. I'll wager that amongst the regular away fans even at 4-1 up they were tempted to cash out on their bet rather than risk not coming out on top. That probably would have seemed a wise move when Cambridge came out in the second half with a new formation. Dominating the early stages, they soon pulled one back and the nerves began to jangle, but unusually for Pompey, fears were soon allayed when we scored a rather comical fifth, Ryan Taylor's misconnection trickling over the line at about the speed of Del and Rodney's Robin Reliant. Matt Tubbs completed the classic hat trick with a left foot shot and I'd just seen the biggest Pompey away win since Noah saw the weather forecast.

We spent half an hour in the supporters club trying not to look happy amongst so many glum faces, then froze to death outside and mulled over one-tooth's loquacious restrictions before our taxi took us back to the hotel. You can say what you like about Premier Inn but having stayed in a few, they are invariably consistent. The rooms are always clean, the televisions invariably work properly, and most particularly, the showers always seem powerful. This attribute was especially welcome this particular evening. After 5 minutes in the hot shower I felt like I'd been in a microwave on Defrost mode, and was ready to hit the town.

In business terms, you can respect the guy who set up the Premier Inn brand, because you get exactly what it says on the tin. On the subject of brand, a recent report suggested that Southampton had the best "up and coming brand" in the Premier League. Unbelievable that it is that someone should even be investing money in something as absurd as ranking football clubs by brand, it does illustrate how Sky money has caused our top flight to turn its back on the bread and butter football fan who really couldn't give a monkeys about their club "brand". Of course immediately following this report, there was an influx of Saints supporters on to the Portsmouth social media football sites crowing about this award, which some clearly felt even out-ranked their most recent piece of silverware, almost their only piece of silverware, the Johnston Paint Trophy. Though when I say supporters I suspect proper Saints fans were a little embarrassed by their apparent elevation to the top of the league for soulless football clubs. Suffice to say that the plastic variety were sent back to their armchairs with taunts about "best brand for selling your best players" and not winning anything.

However, I digress, though it may happen quite a lot in this book. Even a quick change meant that we were late meeting up with the others. We made up our drinking time quickly in the splendid Bath House in Cambridge, where going through the real ale taps meant a certain headache the next morning. The Isle of Wight boys appeared briefly with their fraudulently obtained bottle of wine still proudly in tow, and we talked to a couple of twenty-something Essex brothers who were working in demolition in Cambridge. They proclaimed our Pompey contingent "proper people" compared to the disdain they showed towards the locals whose city they were gradually decimating with more precision than the Luftwaffe.

One of the two brothers was extremely drunk. Well, actually, they were both extremely drunk but he was the more pissed of the two. He had obviously taken a bit of a shine to our Nicola, and discovering that Paddy was her younger brother, he grilled him for personal information. He wanted to know her star sign, which Paddy didn't know, but eventually plumped for her middle name which is Leigh. He sidled up to her confidently albeit unsteadily like a man out of TOWIE and began a conversation in which every question would have an answer which contained the word Leigh. He said his favourite actress was Vivienne Leigh – wasn't she great in Gone With The Wind – and how Janet Leigh shouldn't have been murdered in Psycho. He asked her if she'd ever been to Leigh on Sea near to where he was born. Paddy and I watched on with amusement and Nicola clearly thought he was bonkers. He carried on undeterred however, clearly trying to create the impression that he had paranormal powers like Dynamo. For my part I was tempted to ask him if he could make Southampton disappear. Eventually he departed quickly with his brother who was getting a flea in his telephone ear for having failed to return home at 3.30 as he had apparently promised.

I looked around our increasingly loud table pondering upon how long I'd known this group of friends and realised that it was over 40 years since we'd all first turned up at the local state Grammar school in 1970 from different feeder schools. We'd not been particular friends until we were about 14 but football had gradually forged a bond. Steve never made the heady heights of what was to prove a highly successful first team (we'd won the Hampshire sixes, runners up in the Hampshire Cup, and were eventually knocked out of the nationals by Millfield, the well-known sports school). Andy played in goal, I was a centre back and Chop was our midfield general and captain. Steve just came along for the celebrations.

Our school, in the north of Portsmouth, had a girls end and a boys end with a sort of no mans land (or to be politically correct, "persons land") in the middle. Mixing was discouraged. However, during the lunch break, fraternisation occurred at "Nora's" sweet and grocery shop opposite, which served as a meeting place. Many a fledgling relationship was forged in Nora's side alley over a quick snog and half a pound of broken biscuits.

As we finished O levels (now GCSEs) the Labour government abolished state Grammars and our two schools merged into one, joined by other kids from what had been secondary moderns. The school retained a sixth form for a few years before being disbanded and we did our A levels at the new school which was simply called Mayfield.

It was in the co-educational sixth form unit that Steve, Andy and Chop cosied up to their future wives, Sue, Bev and Toni respectively. Sue and Bev were best friends, and Chop had actually been an item with Toni since the age of about 14, the broken biscuits seemingly acting as an aphrodisiac upon them from an earlier age.

The exception to this incestuous group was Michelle. I'd met her while at University (Ok Polytechnic to be precise, my A levels were shite) in Newcastle. She was a true Geordie, apart from the fact that her fanatical Magpies dad – at least in his earlier days – had not instilled in her any particular affection for football. We got married in 1981 notwithstanding, spent 6 months on the Old King Cole living in an 8th storey Council flat on the Scotswood Road, and then moved back down to Pompey when we both managed to get jobs back down south.

We'd all been married for over 30 years which seems quite a rare statistic these days.

My daughter Nicola –unlike her mum – had football instilled in her from an early age. At the age of 13 she could recite every first and second division football ground. At various times throughout childhood she and her two brothers had accompanied me to Fratton Park as season ticket holders.

Dan, my middle son, now had a job requiring him to work Saturdays so he had to abandon his season ticket and Paddy, my youngest, had toddled off to experience university life (seemingly with few lectures) at Nottingham. He'd now finished but had plans to travel, though he got to most home matches after he returned to Pompey.

Nicola was now living with her football atheist partner, but renewed her season ticket year on year with me. I remember Michelle once saying that she was looking forward to Nicola returning from University because the conversation around the dinner table might turn to something other than football and golf. She was right. When Nicola came home, she extended it to cricket, even to the extent that she planned a few months away travelling (which sadly for various reasons never happened) which centred on the England Ashes series in Australia.

We were later joined in the pub by Belinda, one of Toni's best friends from school, and Brad, her husband, both of whom joined us occasionally on match days away.

Having gorged on the hospitality, us posh people were not bothered about eating in the evening, apart from the usual packets of crisps. As the evening drew out, however, I observed one of those things that demonstrates the "women from Venus, men from Mars" theory. Chop and Steve were in full flow on the beer and Chop was clearly determined to sample every variety of hand-pulled beer in the pub. Toni and Sue were gradually becoming more and more grumpy as the evening wore on. They wanted to eat and Chop's suggestion of twelve packets of Scampi Fries, followed by a Pork Scratchings dessert, did not quite hit the spot. I've noticed this with nearly all of my friends. Once on the beer, men can go a whole evening without proper food and can happily go to bed on a bag of chips and curry sauce after closing time. Women however need to eat or they become fractious, like they are in the middle of some pre-menstrual food deprivation, and this was clearly evident in the Bath House. Chop had become rather attached to his bar stool but at about 9.15 he decided to earn the brownie points he had long earlier forfeited , and went to the bar for a menu, hoping to achieve the dual benefit of a less grumpy wife and being able to stay put to sample the rest of the ale on offer. By the time menu choices were made and he went to the bar to order, they had stopped serving food. Delivering this message to the wives resulted in Medusa like stares and he and Steve, realising that they might have to sew bits back on if they tarried any longer, disappeared with their women off to Prezzo for pizza and bottles of beer at triple the price.

Returning to our hotel, and ready to hit my £14.50 share of our Premier Inn bed we encountered the Pompey chairman, Ian McInnes, trotting off to his bed with his wife and a bottle of wine. Presumably he'd won the quiz in the boardroom as well. Mr. McInnes and his fellow board members had been getting a lot of stick, being blamed as amateurs at running a football club along with their appointed CEO Mark Catlin. This puzzled me immensely. Most of these guys were successful local businessmen with an affinity to their local football club. They had put in large sums of their personal money to join with the fans trust in saving the club from extinction. Each of them ran businesses which probably individually exceeded the turnover of the football club whose direction they were collectively steering. Yet they were apparently at fault for our lowly league position and just about everything else, primarily for appointing a manager who was now struggling to make an impact on League Two. In truth, their previous managerial appointment, a guy called Ritchie Barker, had been an absolute disaster. However when long serving player and youth team coach Andy Awford had stepped into the breach as his successor and ran up a string of wins to save us from possible relegation the season before, it seemed a no-brainer to 99% of fans (and presumably the Board) that his appointment as manager should be confirmed over the summer. About 49% of that 99% were now calling the same man Andy Awful, and accusing the Directors of being naïve in appointing a manager without experience. As they say, hindsight is a wonderful thing. I suspected that half of these critics felt qualified to advise on this subject as a result of being treasurer of the pub darts team or an esteemed member of the local Scout group committee, but I imagined it must be pretty galling for the people running the club to sustain this criticism.

We exchanged pleasantries for a couple of minutes before Mr. McInnes disappeared into the lift with a shout of "sack the Board". We assumed, when he came down to breakfast the following morning, that his decision to stay in Cambridge had been made late in a moment of euphoria because he was wearing the same clothes as the night before. He'd presumably also paid more than £14.50 for his share of the bed but we figured he could afford it.

We shot off to watch the Football League show, a programme which claimed the distinction of being able to show an 8 – goal fest in under 30 seconds. Even on Match of the Day the most dire 0-0 draw is given more airtime.

Still, a brilliant Saturday and a definite departure from our other Pompey away day experiences both before and after.

CHAPTER TWO

SOUTHEND

Most of our other awayday experiences in the 2014/15 season proved disappointing.

We had started the season well with three wins and a draw in our first four matches. The bookies had made us favourites for the title purely on the strength of our fan base and attendances but the initial expectation and euphoria had soon evaporated as the inability to win away kicked in. We had apparently been fortunate to win our second away league game at Oxford with a last minute goal but a pointless away drought ensued. Our first away game of the season had resulted in a draw against an Exeter team with a transfer embargo, who even named their manager Paul Tisdale on the bench. As a manager he wore a flat cap on the touchline. I wondered if he'd wear it on the pitch if called upon.

I like Paul Tisdale as a League Two manager. His teams play proper football rather than hump and lump. I hoped that he'd get the job when we appointed Barker; he was interviewed but the fact that Barker (or Barking as he became known to the supporters) had Steve Coppell as his mentor seemed to hold more water for the Board.

Various defeats away had followed for us as our frailties had been emphasised but Pompey fans, like Mr. Micawber, always take the view that something will turn up. On reflection it may have also been as well if our financial managers in the Premier League had borne in mind Mr. Micawber's words that income at twenty pounds and expenditure at twenty pounds and sixpence equals misery. Ironic really that the words were scribed by Charles Dickens, Portsmouth's most famous inhabitant.

With misplaced optimism we decide to go to Southend in September. They were managed by Phil Brown – he of the permatan and forever humiliated by Jimmy Bullard's goal celebration at Hull when he replicated the finger-wagging half time team talk which Brown Phil had given on the pitch a couple of weeks earlier.

Steve offered to drive to the game and we were up and back on the same day. No overnight guest house stays or jellied eels on the seafront. It was full on get to the game, couple of pints, celebrate a win and get the hell out of there. Paddy joined us for the experience.

Setting off about 10.30 we made great time until arriving at the Essex coast and more particularly Southend itself which clearly employs the same traffic management expert as Cambridge. We parked up about 1pm and proceeded to The Railway, which was said to be one of a number of away fans friendly pubs in Southend. Unfortunately the local police had made an executive decision to make all but one of the pubs home fans only. I guessed that this was because they were expecting an invasion from pretty much the biggest away following in League Two (along with Luton). We'd planned to meet an old school mate Tigger at the Railway. He'd moved to Southend many years earlier to work closer to London. Best laid plans gone to ruin, we never saw him from start to finish either inside or outside the ground, and at 19 stone, Tigger's hard to miss. Thanks must go to Southend constabulary for this.

We were directed to the only pub admitting away fans and found the Blue Boar which was packed out with Portsmouth supporters. As you'd expect it took hours to get a beer and the place was heaving both inside and out on the street. We bought a double round, stood Steve a couple of shandies for driving and egressed on to the packed pavement.

The Blue Boar was on a main bus route out of Southend and this created some amusing moments. It was right on a crossroads with traffic lights so the buses would stop outside of a pub containing raucous but friendly away supporters, many of whom like us were standing outside. As the buses approached the lights, in slow moving traffic, the mob would shout OOOOOOOOOOOOOOOOOH as the lights went from green to red. Buses stood stationary at the lights and this provided some interesting people watching. Some bus occupants looked at the crowd outside of the pub like they were refugees from a Calais immigrant camp. Others looked slightly intimidated – and I could understand why – but some were up for a bit of banter, exchanging gestures with the away fans. One rather fat and bald middle aged fan would run out and wiggle his enormous beer belly next to the bus window. On one occasion he did it to a woman pensioner who looked about 85. Unlike some of her fellow bussers she waved him away with contempt and a furtive smile which said "you are awful but I like you".

Unlike their superiors who had made the ridiculous decision to try to herd half of Portsmouth into one pub, the police outside the pub were excellent. They showed an uncanny ability to recognise what was harmless fun and what had the potential to escalate into something more intimidating. Perhaps their superiors should promote them and demote themselves.

It was outside the Blue Boar that I had the horrible experience of looking into the pub window and realising that

John Westwood (yes, him with the clown shoes, the hat and the bell) was sat in the pub window with the crease of his arse hanging out of his trousers. I'd sat in close proximity to John before. In the Premier League days I sat behind him at both Newcastle and Everton. At Newcastle I wondered he could stand up he was so drunk and at Everton he was eventually chucked out of the ground after repeatedly making rude gestures to the Everton fans with some sort of giant phallus he was carrying under his raincoat. He couldn't really complain as he'd been warned several times and the stewards had seemed desperate not to kick him out..

Anyway, I had the opportunity to get a closer look at his hat as I looked through the window of the Blue Boar. Someone had stuck onto it one of those memos you get at airports when they refuse to take hazardous luggage. Next to the section showing "reason for refusal" someone had written "Twat". He seemed to carry this slur with pride.

Match time was getting close and we needed to eat. We crossed the road to a fish shop with a long queue which nonetheless reduced quickly and efficiently. Whilst in the queue we talked turkey with a couple of Southend supporters, anticipating the match ahead and swapping information about our best players. You wouldn't find a Man City fan stood in a fish shop queue with a Liverpool fan saying "You won't know but we've got a cracking number 9 called Aguero". We talked about our up and coming Jed Wallace and they raved about their 'keeper. It was all pretty civilised and friendly. They gave a mention to West Ham but never gave any hint that they would think of supporting anyone other than Southend. I liked and respected that. The fish and chips were, by the way, as good as I've had anywhere.

I think Paddy had a large portion. This may explain why he is six foot five when none of his parents or grandparents managed to get close to six feet. I see this regularly, inexplicably tall kids to ridiculously small parents. Over the years I've formed a theory that it comes down to junk food. My generation was brought up on meat and two veg, even more so the generation before us. I once remember in the early 70s my mum telling her aunt that there was a café in central Portsmouth which had put Lasagne on the menu and she should give it a try when she was next out shopping. In those days Lasagne was not a standard part of a pub menu and was actually almost mysteriously exotic. Anyway when she next popped in the aunt told my mum "I tried that Lassannee" (as she described it). It was alright, but you don't get no spuds"

Modern day kids are fed more carbs, eat more takeaways, and drink more fizzy and sugary drinks. In some it shows in obesity but in others in height. So my theory is it's all down to less fruit and veg and more junk food.

We got to Roots Hall which is slightly larger than the average League two ground though it was still difficult to envisage that it had a 12,000 capacity. The Pompey end had not sold out completely and we were told by the stewards that we could pretty much sit where we wanted. I bet that isn't a phrase that passes the lips of the stewards at the Emirates.

The ground itself was neat and compact. The away end was deeper than many League two grounds but the view was on the whole good. The stand to our left contained the hospitality areas, which looked, like most League Two grounds, to be occupied by Bob's Tyre Services rather than Accenture or PWC. To our right was a stand which looked like an extended allotment shack, and it was here that the home drummer was positioned, presumably so located to impose maximum irritation on the away supporters.

The game itself was unbelievably dull. Our play lacked any real cohesion and we were pretty toothless. Southend were not a great deal better but you could see them winning this one. Even Jed was off colour. It was no surprise when their bulky centre forward Barry Corr put Southend ahead as we failed to deal with a corner early in the second half. He'd inflicted pain at Fratton Park the year previous and you always felt that it was going to happen again. They got a second when they broke away following a corner at our end of the ground and it was game over. Our manager proceeded to put on two diminutive subs against a strong physical side in a moment of tactical nous which had about a 1% chance of producing a result.

Just along from us was a girl/woman, probably early twenties, who had been giving it her all in the singing stakes. She seemed to be there with her dad who looked like he could probably handle himself. When the second goal went in, dad looked to have left in disgust, but his daughter (I suppose it could have been his girlfriend but unlikely) stayed on. Whilst the singing from the Pompey end ground to a virtual halt in a sea of despair, she was stood on her seat still belting it out like Katharine Jenkins at the Cup Final. A bunch of lads behind her started to give her a bit of friendly stick, and she reacted by telling them to "Fucking get behind the team". Knowing this particular cause was lost, they resorted to a chorus of "Get your tits out for the lads" which prompted from her an invitation to "fuck off". Bless her, she kept going to the end. In Pompey parlance she would be described as a "mushbird". Broadly, that means that she's a girl who can mix it with the blokes and hold her own verbally. It's not necessarily a derogatory term. Technically, you could have a bum like Jennifer Lopez and still be a mushbird. That said, if, like so many people these days, you can be subjectively hurt and humiliated at anything, you'd be disqualified from mushbird status. Mushbirds don't seek compensation for anything. It's a phrase which I think is unique to Pompey, mind. My Nicola would take a certain pride in being elected to Mushbird ranks.

Here is an example of two mushbirds having a conversation overheard in Kwikimart in Buckland:-

"I don't want another steady boyfriend for now, I wanna play the field"

"Nothing wrong with playing the field, but you don't have to be the fucking field, you slag".

In fairness, notwithstanding that a mushbird can have Jennifer Lopez's rear, Jennifer Aniston's visage and a Baywatch body and without being disrespectful to our local women folk, it would be harder for a cameraman to scan our crowd to focus on the best looking women than scanning the Sweden end at the World Cup.

We trooped away from Roots Hall depressed and made our way back to the car. This result had put Southend into the promotion frame which in a way was even more depressing since they really weren't much better than us. We weren't inclined to hang around for a post-match debate with the guys from the fish shop queue. We never found out if their keeper was as good as they said because he spent most of the game filing his fingernails.

We drove out along Southend seafront. It was like going back in time with the jellied eels, amusement arcades and chip shops. The beach looked trim enough but I couldn't get out of my mind the jolly boys outing special of Only Fools and Horses. The thing that spoiled the view for me was the ugly spectre of the Shoeburyness power station which dominated the horizon. It was impossible not to be drawn to it. I'd always wondered why some people would spend seven figures to buy a mansion at Warsash, which is in a Southampton postcode, just to have a view of Fawley Oil Refinery. This was much the same.

As we got away from the main centre, there was some imposing property on the seafront, but give me a view of the Isle of Wight over a view of a power station any day.

The journey home proved quicker than the outward journey. The only disconcerting moment was mild vertigo as we went over the Dartford Bridge.

CHAPTER THREE

CHELTENHAM

S adly, our Southend experience dissuaded us from any away trips in October or November, as our miserable winless away run continued. I had however already devised a cunning plan for a pre-Christmas away weekend in Cheltenham and this was our next foray into away travel.

Peter and Diane have become perhaps our closest friends. They live where we have lived for the last 25 years and our kids were best friends at school. Pete and I both like good beer and good food, the women like good wine and good food and our wives are both Northerners. Well in fact so is Pete. They come from St. Helens and both support Everton, the fact that one is Catholic and the other Protestant being irrelevant, quite rightly. Pete started to come to Pompey home games when it became difficult to get tickets for Everton's London away matches. He sort of adopted us as a second team having experienced the Fratton Park atmosphere as we rose from the second division (no, it isn't the bloody Championship) to the top flight. Together with a couple of other friends, Dave and Sally, we'd done an away weekend every year we were in the top flight. We did Wigan one year, Hull another, Newcastle, and most regularly of all Everton.

I recall our weekend in Wigan with some surprise at the

sentiments of one of the locals. Checking into our hotel the youngish local lad on reception asked the purpose of our visit. We told him we were up for the match the following day. "I hope you beat them" he replied "Rugby town, this".

Our very last trip to Goodison before we were ejected from the Premier League also brings back memories. We had already pretty much gone into financial meltdown. We had a bunch of journeyman professionals. But somehow we managed to beat star studded Harry Redknapp managed Tottenham in the semi final of the FA Cup to make the final against Chelsea. It was to be played the following Saturday but first we had to bow out of the top league, long ago relegated, in a final away game against Everton.

Conscious of the occasion, the fans dressed up for the occasion. There were Orville outfits, superheroes and a vast number of bewigged 118 lookalikes. The game itself was complete garbage but the fun started after half time. Last game of the season and it was clearly Health and Safety time. Over the loudspeaker came a scouse voice "Operation Goodison exercise". We waited for some sort of steward activity but nothing happened at all. Five minutes later the same announcement came over the tannoy, again without any sign of action. Our section broke into a rendering of "Where is your exercise, where is your exercise?" to the tune of Verdi's drinking song from La Traviata. Five minutes later the same announcement once again; on this occasion 2,000 away fans in a mixture of wigs and duck outfits performed star jumps in front of their seats. Even the Everton fans applauded the terrace humour, well it wasn't hard to take your eyes off the game. Incidentally we lost to a Johnny Heltsinger thunderbolt in the last minute but the good wishes and handshakes we got for the following week's Cup final as we walked away from the ground will forever endear me to Everton fans. Ever presents in our top league for longer than nearly everyone, they nonetheless ain't got airs and graces. Proper football club in my opinion.

Oh and of course we lost the Cup Final the following week. Chelsea put splinters in the Pompey woodwork before we finally lost to a Drogba fee kick after Kevin Boateng (the artist known as Prince) missed a penalty for us before they scored.

Anyway, having trawled the fixture list, I plumped for Cheltenham. I had established that (supposedly, and if you trust city council websites, explicitly) it had a thriving Christmas market, they were languishing in League Two's nether regions, and I smelled a rare away victory. Tickets were purchased at modest cost, and we booked into Holiday Inn by Express also at modest cost. Like the Premier Inn chain, you know what you're going to get and the price is fair.

Having a POETS day from work (for those who don't know, that is "piss off early tomorrow's Saturday") we finally got away about 3pm on the Friday and missed most of the traffic. It was as we got past Swindon that I realised that my satnav was hopelessly out of date. Driving along a dual carriageway without roundabouts I was repeatedly advised that at the roundabout I should take the second exit. The road had clearly been updated since 2008 and Sarah, my satnav guide, was going apoplectic. I call her Sarah because I once knew a very assertive woman called Sarah with a voice similar to my satnav narrator. The "recalculating" icon appeared regularly on my screen as I flew at 70 mph across roundabouts that no longer existed. I felt like Starsky and Hutch on one of their car chases – and yes, for the record, I did once have a Starsky and Hutch cardigan. We made Cheltenham in two hours.

A quick examination of the room for CIA bugs (not that I'm paranoid) and we hit the town. Our first task was to locate the expansive Christmas market. Stumbling upon a couple of wooden shacks but nothing more, we soon gave up and decided to explore the hostelries of Cheltenham. First however we felt we needed a snack, and one of the shacks was selling home made burgers at a fiver a throw. They looked good, and there were several basic and more exotic varieties. For my part I went for the Scimitar-horned Oryx burger, or something like that; it was delicious, though tasted really like it was just beef. It was about 6 months later that I visited Marwell safari park and felt a guilt rush when I read a plaque that the Scimitar-horned Oryx was now extinct in the wild. I like my meat rare but not that rare.

We strolled down to Montpellier, the posh bit, and looked at the restaurant menus. This part of Cheltenham has some fantastic looking restaurants with appealing menus. Anything which says that it's served with jus floats my boat and I was regretting the fact that we'd made a fairly last minute decision to go to Cheltenham which meant that the best restaurants were already booked up. Whilst I don't like feeling ripped off I'm always prepared to pay for quality over quantity. As it happened, I'd pre-booked a Turkish restaurant nearer our hotel that Trip Advisor reviews had recommended. The fact that I had a Gourmet Society card which gave us 25% off the total bill was immaterial to our decision to eat there.

We worked our way back from Montpellier to our hotel and I liked Cheltenham more and more. The pubs were busy and the whole ambience of the place was endearing. It felt like an unpretentious university town, with a majority of the patrons in open-toed sandals in the middle of winter discussing current affairs. They weren't – in open toed sandals I mean – but they might have been. There was a choice of good beer in every pub. We visited about four and could have gone through the taps in an evening at any of them. One of the quieter more "local" alehouses we visited had walls devoted to pictures and cuttings of the Cheltenham racing festival over the years. It was like heaven. Imagine going to a museum you've always wanted to visit but with the added bonus of walking around it with a pint of best bitter, and not paying an entry fee.

Diane and Michelle were by now getting grumpy (see chapter one) and we made our way to the Turkish restaurant. We were warmly welcomed and handed a menu where the price of the food was astonishingly good value. I reckoned I could have handed over one of my old school dinner tickets in exchange for 3 courses. We ordered beer and wine, starters and mains, all of which were fine and when the bill came I don't think (with my cheapskate money off card) it came to more than £25 a couple. For all of that, I can't say Turkish cuisine really grabs me. I've never been in an expensive Turkish restaurant but I just wouldn't eat Turkish in preference to Italian, Spanish, French or even English. But you can't knock them for value.

We retired to our hotel. It looked like an office Christmas party was in full flow. Women who spent their whole year in leggings had decided that it was appropriate to put on their best party dresses for the benefit of men that they probably didn't like very much, and men who wore suits for most of the year were wearing jeans. Well, apart from one guy. His suit was white and it was patterned with what were effectively prints of newspaper cuttings. At first I thought it was a sort of liquorice allsort suit but on closer examination realised that it was just horrible. The funny thing was that he obviously felt that it gave him pulling power as he never took off the jacket even though it was like a sauna in the hotel. I tried to get close enough to read what the newspaper print said but had to back off when I realised that to finish the story I would have to put my face close to his groin. Undoubtedly, that was his cunning plan. I don't think he had in mind that it would be an overweight 55 year old male though.

Dispassionately watching people on a night out is great entertainment.. I knew exactly who he fancied and who he was trying to pull. I was outside having a smoke when the woman's husband turned up to collect her. Liquorice Allsort man came out and greeted him like a long lost friend. I would have wagered that an hour earlier, he'd have paid for a rack rate double room just for half an hour's rumpy-pumpy with her.

The party ended and no longer having the amusement of watching a walking Sunday People trying to tap off, we finished our drinks and retired for the night, agreeing to go out orienteering for the elusive market the following morning. After a breakfast served in a breakfast area which I thought might have something in common with the mess at Camp Bastion, we set off to discover what the permanent and temporary retail offer of Cheltenham had in store. In fact, it's a pleasant town with a city centre that could put much bigger places (like Portsmouth in particular) to shame. For Pompey read Shoezone, for Cheltenham read Jones the Bootmaker. We stumbled on the same wooden shacks from the night before, now fully open, and treated ourselves to a mid-morning mulled wine. There was also an interesting cheese stall, and I made a beeline for it. There were little taster samples of the different cheeses and after testing each one critically like John Torode on Masterchef, I selected the chilli and lime cheddar as the first purchase of my annual Christmas cheesefest. About an hour later the sample was still burning my lips.

Another reason for making a beeline for the cheese stall was that I'd noticed a Radley store, which the cheese stall obscured from view. Now I have a wife who has a wardrobe of different coloured Radley handbags, all varied in size. It's my theory that the scotty dogs on these handbags have a breeding programme going on in her wardrobe because suddenly a new handbag, in a colour I've not seen before, will unexpectedly appear. We had been on holiday in Spain for Michelle's birthday a couple of months earlier and she still hadn't had a present. In fairness she'd had a card but it was in Spanish and had been bought at little expense at the local Chinese Hypermarket, as I'd forgotten to take an English version in my luggage. If she saw the Radley store I'm sure the presentless recent birthday would be brought up.

I walked briskly away from the cheese stall with my purchase, thinking that I'd successfully manoeuvred away from Radley but Michelle's nose suddenly twitched and I realised that she'd caught the scent of leather. I was dragged backwards into the shop and a rather large bag was selected for purchase when we'd finished our search for the source of the Nile, otherwise known as the Cheltenham Christmas market. Eventually we realised that we had walked past it on the other side of the road the previous night on our visit to Montpellier, so we went to the far end and strolled back along it in the direction of our hotel.

On the basis that this had ostensibly been the prompt for our Cheltenham trip, or at least so the ladies believed, the Christmas market was actually a little disappointing. Much as I admire the craft skills of people who sit at home in their various cottage industries making pottery Peter Rabbit brooches or blown glass geese, it's rare that I ever see anything which will realistically be of practical use. There were lots of people smiling, looking and pointing at the merchandise, but not much of it seemed to be getting sold. I window-shopped through the market without putting my hand in my pocket, conscious of the stress which the forthcoming Radley purchase would cause to my credit card. As we re-entered the Radley shop I saw another chap in a replica Pompey shirt supervising the gift-wrapping of his purchase and figured that his wife had only got a birthday card in Spanish as well.

It was time to start on our pre-match pub crawl to the game, but as it happened we spent an hour and a half before 3 o'clock in the same place. This was explained by the fact that we came upon possibly the best pub I've come across close to a football ground. It wasn't on the main drag to anywhere but on a back street close to the ground.

It was long and narrow, with what seemed a comparatively small capacity until you walked to the toilets, when you realised that it was a bit of a tardis with a further open air bit at the back, primarily populated by those nasty smokers. There was a great selection of real ale and the staff were friendly. A fairly even number of home and away fans, and locals with no football interest whatsoever, all mixed harmoniously aided by the warmth of the pub and the variety of the ale. My instinctive affection for the place was further enhanced when I bought the first round and was directed by the landlord to an urn of free food which they had laid on for the lunchtime drinkers, and we were told to help ourselves. It wasn't a culinary masterpiece, but a polystyrene bowl of Chorizo and bean casserole with crusty bread soaked up the splendid beer just right. We met and chatted with a couple of people we knew from Portsmouth and whiled away a very pleasant hour or two before the main event. The name of this great little pub is the Kemble Arms brewery. It's just a shame that Cheltenham's relegation meant that I wouldn't be back for at least a year. The Football League's loss is the Conference's/ National League's gain.

Cheltenham's ground, at Whaddon Road (now called The Abbey Stadium), is extremely quaint. None of the stands would infringe the neighbours' right to light or air. We took our seats in row E which was about halfway back. Unlike had I been in the away end at St. James's Park (Newcastle, not Exeter) the vertigo I experienced on the Dartford Bridge wasn't about to be repeated as I climbed the steps to my seat. It was a cold crisp and clear winter's day and as I looked above the stand at the other end of the pitch I could see the Cotswold Hills framing the view. It was a far cry from Old Trafford.

The first half saw the home side kicking into the goal at

our end of the pitch. Which meant that we were kicking into the goal at the other end. Or that was how I saw it. Seemingly, our players didn't, or at least didn't realise that the goal is in the centre rather than near the corner flag. Cheltenham weren't much better, and chances were few and far between. I was a little embarrassed that I'd subjected friends to the spectacle but it was their first experience of League Two and I got away with it purely because of the novelty value.

Just before half time one of the home side toddled into our penalty box and a drop of his shoulder, hardly of Messi proportions, sent three of our defenders onto their arses like Weebles that wobbled but did fall down. As he then lashed the ball past our 'keeper I sighed and suggested to Pete that we indulge Cheltenham Town FC by testing the culinary delights of their pies which looked quite tasty. Unfortunately, the more experienced and hardy supporters knew that clubs under-cater for Pompey numbers. By the time we got to the front of the queue there was nothing left but very average burgers, though in tribute to our early football-watching days we bought 4 Bovrils to wash them down.

You could pretty much do what you liked. There were conversations and reunions going on in the level part of terracing behind the goal and in the aisles. No officious stewards telling you to move because you're blocking something or other. 'Elf and Safety may be alive and kicking in the Premiership and I suppose in view of the size of the crowds necessarily so, but you can have a good old chinwag anywhere at Cheltenham's ground. Which presumably explained that when a dozen or so Cheltenham fans in Santa outfits ran across the pitch to the halfway line, the stewards barely moved. I can't say that I saw the Santas again but I bet they didn't get banning orders. If they did, Cheltenham wouldn't have a quorum for the next game.

For once, the half-time team talk seemed to have

invigorated Pompey and they emerged with what looked like an appetite for football which had been sadly lacking in the first half.

We exerted severe pressure and created a couple of chances which weren't taken, before Nigel Atangana, playing in an unusual position for him behind the front two, curled in a beauty off the underside of the bar. We looked dominant and in control. Looking back, we should have buried this game, but the story of our season was that we were more likely to go on to lose games we were drawing than win them. Cheltenham were relegated to the Conference at the end of the season and we really should have picked up 3 points here.

We got back to the hotel by a rather circuitous route which somehow bypassed the landmarks we'd seen walking to the ground, but an hour and a hot shower later we exited the hotel to once again discover the delights of Cheltenham.

Our first stop was at The Bank or something like that, which was a Wetherspoons pub. They were selling jugs of mulled wine for about 20p, a bargain that was impossible to resist. The pub, like most Wetherspoons, had been converted from an old building that had probably been an office, a department store, or most probably in view of its' name, a bank. Notwithstanding its' size, which was substantial, it was hard to find a table, the pre-Christmas revellers being out in force.

Having seen off our jug of mulled wine, we moved on to our restaurant of choice for the evening, Jamie's Italian. Well, I say restaurant of choice, but in fact it was more like Hobsons Choice because Cheltenham was seemingly rammed with pre-bookings and there was little left on offer. We were slightly early and our table wasn't quite ready, so we were shown upstairs to a small bar and settled down for an aperitif, otherwise known as beer.

The restaurant had formerly been the Courthouse and

had been sympathetically adapted. I always thinks it helps the atmosphere of a restaurant or pub if it has a theme of some sort. For that reason and although I find the food average, a trip to Frankie and Bennies always makes me feel like I've been taken back in time to 1920s America, with pictures of Babe Ruth or his contemporaries smothering the walls and the, admittedly piped, period music.

In Cheltenham, Jamie's even had old courthouse relics behind toughened glass, visible on a trip to the toilets, and the high ceilings conjured up thoughts of Hanging Judges and black caps. I wondered how many lives had been sentenced to end in this building.

Expecting to be summoned to dinner by a gavel, I was brought back to life by a cordial smiling waitress who led us to our table. I was further brought back to reality by the menu. Now I like Jamie Oliver from what I've seen of him on TV, and his ideas on food, but can't help feeling that his restaurants don't live up to his aspirations. I have eaten in three different Jamie's now and on each occasion have struggled to find anything which really appeals from the menu. And this is from a man whose only food aversion is to any sign of beetroot on a plate. With his culinary ideals, one might expect the chefs in each of Jamie's restaurants to be given a much freer rein to create an individual specials board but the off-menu choices were equally as uninspiring. It was a pleasant enough evening in good company in a restaurant with a lively atmosphere but I can't for one moment remember what I had to eat. That may have been partly explained by the two bottles of Sauvignon Blanc we mullered in between courses.

Emerging into the Cheltenham night we lazily stepped into the pub next door for a final nightcap. I chewed the fat for a while with the bouncer on the door who I suspected was not overstretched by the middle-class Cheltenham clientele, other than with the Irish invasion in the week of the

Cheltenham racing festival, though he was also pretty scathing of Gloucester and anyone from inside its' city boundaries, and I realised that even in the Cotswolds, inter-city rivalry is alive and well.

A good night's kip and a quick foray into Camp Bastion once more the following morning, and we were ready to hit the road and plough through the mystic roundabouts on the way to Swindon. A couple of hours later we were home and there was still enough time to prep Sunday dinner.

It had been a great weekend. How sad in a way that Cheltenham no longer formed part of the 92.

CHAPTER 4

DAGENHAM

There were few opportunities to get away over Christmas 2014 and in early January 2015 the season of woe continued as we were knocked out of the FA Cup by non-league Aldershot. So, yet to experience the Cambridge turnaround, I really can't remember why we were even remotely tempted to get tickets for Dagenham and Redbridge during a cold snap in early February.

Having looked at the train timetable, however, Paddy worked out that with permission to work his lunch hour, he could get away from work in just about sufficient time for us to make the game. We were joined by his two best mates Jack and Kieran, both season ticket holders.

We arranged to meet at Petersfield station in time to catch the 16.57 fast train to Waterloo. Fifty seven minutes past the hour is a fairly well-known time for Pompey fans travelling away, though from Portsmouth rather than Petersfield. Back in the 70s it was the train caught by the Pompey "crew", the 657. Most of these guys were my contemporaries or at least about 4 or 5 years older. I never caught that particular train being somewhat squeamish of blood but I did know a few people who did, and still have the scars from playing local football against a number of others.

I arrived in plenty of time having been dropped off by Michelle. The station car park was pretty packed and I feared that Paddy would struggle to find a space, which was worrying as he was already going to be cutting it fine. There was one space left in the station car park and I was hoping that a few people would have skived off early from work, caught an early train back from Waterloo, and would free up a few spaces. The Waterloo train came through, people exited and walked through the car park but none seemed to have parked there. The one solitary space remained. I was considering commandeering some cones, and placing them in front of the space, a bit like some people who think they own the 12 foot of parking space outside of their terraced houses in Pompey. But before I could stand in front of the space with my arms folded menacingly, a small Hyundai drove into the car park and took the spot. An ethnic oriental man, of modest years, emerged and walked into the station. The last space had gone, and I was becoming uncharacteristically agitated at the possibility of us missing the train, disrupting my carefully planned schedule.

What followed over the next 15 minutes was quite bizarre. The lad would suddenly reappear, and walk back to his car. Thinking that maybe he had just parked up to buy a ticket for the following day, I was bemused to note that he just went back to his car and re-parked it in the same spot. He did this on no less than three occasions. It was as if he was paranoid that he'd maybe straddled two spaces and would get fined; or perhaps had some sort of obsessive compulsive disorder that meant that he had to be satisfied that he had parked exactly parallel to the lines in the bay. Either way, it was strange to say the least.

Jack and Kieran arrived, laden down by a Tesco meal deal. I bought a coffee and lived dangerously by having a smoke within a foot of the no smoking zone adjacent to the platform. This is probably the nearest I've ever come to breaking the law.

Our plans did not take into account South West trains. I'd worked out that with a fair wind we could jump on Underground connections and get to Dagenham station by about 7, in plenty of time for a quick pint before the game. In fact my planning had almost reached Overlord proportions. Unfortunately the first timetable hitch was that the 16.57 was cancelled. No announcement or apology; the 16.57 changed from being the "first" train to just be "cancelled". I wondered what reaction I would get from a client turning up for a 12.00 appointment to be told without any explanation that it had just been cancelled. I made a note to complain to the Customer Services manager at South-West trains, otherwise known as Andy.

As it turned out, the cancellation did not matter because Paddy was late anyway. The next train from Waterloo had evicted commuters who had parked in the car park and spaces magically appeared for his late arrival at 17.05, in time for the next train which was due to arrive at 17.10. In fact that train was also late, but when we jumped on it at 17.20, the announcement apologised for the delay in its arrival (a first on South West Trains) but confidently expected to make up the time to arrive at Waterloo at 18.27, which should have allowed ample time to get across London for kick off. I ticked off stage one of the journey with an almost Captain Mainwaring like efficiency.

We fair bombed through to Surbiton and then stopped. Wondering what was going on, an announcement finally came over to the effect that Waterloo was "blocked" and the train wasn't going any further. No further explanation. Had an earlier train had a toilet breakdown and left a ton of turds on the line at Vauxhall? Or maybe there was a suicide? Perhaps terrorists had sabotaged the points. We were never to find out. All we knew was that the Guard was racing through the train excitedly, screaming "Raus, Raus" at the passengers (well, something like that. Get out in railway-speak.). Fearing that we would end up in South West Trains personalised version of Guantanamo Bay if we resisted and stayed put, we jumped off the train and considered our options.

Now this is where being an old fart with a few boy scout badges comes into its own. I reckoned if we could get to Clapham Junction we'd have a range of options. Being the saddo anorak that knows all the colours of the London underground occasionally has its advantages. I gave the wet behind the ears youngsters a variety of options. We could perhaps forget about the football and visit the set of The Good Life. We could go to Turnham Green or somewhere with an equally endearing name, and change at Piccadilly, or we could get off at Wimbledon, walk to the nearest tube station and a couple of changes later we might make Dagenham before midnight. In contrast, Jack in particular, whose eyes had not left his 'phone in the previous half hour, was now completely lost without a signal . They were stranded without wifi for their 'phones and I felt like a veritable Bear Grylls, saving them from death in the suburbs of South London with my superior survival skills.

We just jumped on the next train that came along.

It arrived on the adjacent platform, and we climbed on excitedly hoping that it would be a Japanese bullet which would propel us to Waterloo in record time but in fact it remained stationary for 15 minutes before setting off into the unknown. It took about 10 minutes before it exceeded the speed of Thomas the Tank Engine. We stopped at various non-league stations, any of which we could be visiting the following season if we didn't buck up, and I made a mental note of their location. When we reached Wimbledon it was an agonising decision whether to hop off and make our way through the underground system, but we were told that Waterloo was no longer blocked and rejoicing that they had obviously cleared the pile of excrement from the line, we stayed put. It may have been a mistake. The train was overtaken by several other trains of the Smart Car train equivalent. We stopped at every minor station into Waterloo. A solitary bloke got off at Earlsfield with one of those collapsible bicycles that we had time to watch him re-assemble before moving off, and we eventually arrived at Waterloo already realising that reaching Dagenham before scheduled kick off time was a forlorn hope. Operation Overlord had turned into Operation Market Garden.

The length of the journey meant that Paddy's legendary bladder problems had surfaced, and further delay was experienced before we jumped on a Jubilee line train to West Ham, where we could make an underground connection to Dagenham. Now there was a time in the 70s that you might expect to be met by the Inter-City firm on West Ham station but clearly Portsmouth fans were no longer on their radar following our plummet through the league, and they saved their energy for Millwall games. Suffice to say that West Ham station was half-deserted as we jumped on a District Line connection to Dagenham East, and eventually arrived at 8.15.

I would love to be able to describe the pre-match entertainment, beer and sustenance that Dagenham has to offer, but to salvage the away experience we had to forego everything. There was no time to admire and select purchases from the Londis store and the alluring smells from The Tasty Plaice were put on the back burner as we sped to the ground as fast as my arthritic knees could carry me. The lads raced ahead, frustrated by having to slow down periodically for me to catch up, with looks which somewhat denigrated my Bear Grylls status, but it's not too far from the station to the ground and we arrived with about 8 minutes of the first half remaining to find the gates locked. We hailed the steward just inside the fence who opened the gates and scrutinised our tickets with intensity. He bore a passing resemblance to the guy who played Blakey in On The Buses. He also clearly relished his responsibilities because he examined each ticket as if we'd just bought them outside from a tout, notwithstanding that Dagenham has a limited fan-base and most of them had stayed at home to watch the latest episode of Eastenders. It took him at least another 5 minutes to admit us to the ground. I wished upon him that his wife looked like Olive.

There were about two minutes of the half remaining. Jack had regained his 'phone signal and had been giving us a running commentary from the Portsmouth News feeds on the train from West Ham to Dagenham. We'd realised that our penetration levels had left a lot to be desired and that we'd been spotted in the Dagenham penalty area on approximately 1.25 occasions in the first 40 minutes. In short the first half had been crap. Weighing up the options, we decided to write off the rest of the first half and descend on the bar and burger area behind the stand. It was the best decision we made all night. This was the highlight of our evening. The pints of beer were already poured ready for consumption, a bit like Wembley but on a smaller scale. The beer queue moved quickly and efficiently and we necked a pint before moving to the food bar. Here we were served burgers of the highest quality, presumably sourced from cows left to roam contentedly, chewing the finest cud that Canvey Island has to offer. They were fantastic, albeit priced at the Fortnum and Mason end of League Two at £4.20. I've never had a better burger inside a football ground.

Thoroughly refreshed we returned to the fray for the second half, and found some seats which bore no resemblance to our seat numbers. Nobody really cared. I got the impression, having exchanged a little chat with the poor suckers who'd watched the first half, that anyone who found their seats taken by imposters would be quite grateful. Anyway, seated in the only stand which hinted at anything other than non-league football, we readied ourselves for the joys to come.

The players emerged for the second half from the extendable plastic tunnel. This is something else which distinguishes League two from its Premier League counterparts. Players have to come out of a tunnel OK? However the fact is that many clubs promoted from the Conference have changing rooms which don't lead directly onto the pitch. So the solution is a plastic tunnel like those that you might buy from Toys r Us as a Christmas present for your kids. After the players get back on to the pitch, or off it at the end of a game, you just push it back ready for the next game. Simples innit as they say. I did wonder, as the players emerged, whether there is some sort of intimidating placard hanging down inside the play tunnel like "This is Victoria Road". Doesn't quite have the same ring as "This is Anfield", though I suspect that if Liverpool had been in the Conference we may have been saying the opposite.

Pompey were fielding an unchanged team with 5 across the back, a couple of holding midfielders, and only three players who could have been tagged remotely offensive, including Ryan Taylor our target man who is ginger. Not that such makes him offensive. Dave Kitson, our only other ginger striker in my memory, was offensive to many of our fans, but only because of the obscene amount of money he squeezed out of the Pompey administration. Much as one could resent Kanu for the similar amount of money for which he held out, at least he gave us a Cup Final winner and a draw against AC Milan. I think I remember seeing Dave Kitson once score at Doncaster.

Anyway, it soon became clear that our tactics were that Ryan would try to get his ginger bonce on any stray throw in, goal kick or other punt upfield, with the onus upon our other striker Matt Tubbs to guess where it was going. Invariably he guessed wrong. Toshack and Keegan they weren't and I doubt if they would have got past the first question in Mr and Mrs.

In short it was dire. The game seemed to hover around

the centre circle in a sort of volleyball style head tennis. The Daggers were awful and we were just as bad. Even Jed was substituted when he couldn't make anything happen. I seem to recall just the one reasonably potent piece of football which released our left back Dan Butler, but he sent his cross into the next parliamentary constituency. Most fans were praying. For the final whistle that is. When it blew, the players clapped the fans and the fans clapped the players (it could only have been for keeping a clean sheet) but the show of mutual admiration was, to say the least, tepid, certainly from the fans perspective. The players disappeared down the re-usable Playzone tunnel and we set off for the station.

We once again escaped confrontation at West Ham station and made good time across London in time to catch the 22.45 from Waterloo, and expecting to be tucked up in bed by midnight. Unfortunately, but perhaps predictably, South West Trains performance on this particular day matched the team we'd gone to support. The inward train limped in 20 minutes late, presumably due to more giant turds on the tracks. Even worse we were told that the train back to Portsmouth was reduced to just 4 carriages. I assumed that this was due to a desire to avoid toilet overload and thus turd turmoil for the following morning's commuter traffic.

That the train was "oversubscribed" is perhaps an understatedly kind way to describe it. The first stretch back to Guildford was jam-packed and there was no possibility of getting a seat. The carriages were a mix of Pompey fans coming back from Dagenham (not many), a few Opera goers (more) and Arsenal fans returning to Guildford from the Emirates on a European night (lots).

I've always wondered whether Guildford has any form of football team and if anyone supports them. Whenever Man Utd played at Pompey the standard Fratton chant to the away supporters was "Fuck off back to Guildford" but I'd never realised how true it was that Guildford was a haven for Premier League wannabe supporters until I got on this train and saw so many Arsenal shirts exit there. I'm assuming that it's the same whenever Chelsea are playing. Guildford football fans probably have the monopoly on 606 phone ins, Howard from Guildford complaining that Arsene Wenger is tactically naïve or Jose Mourinho will never win another Champions League until he signs Lionel Messi. I'll say this for them, they sure know their onions in Guildford.

Following the Gunner exodus, the train thinned out, and a seat was procured opposite a couple who'd been to the opera. I thought of singing the Triumphal March from Aida – a popular favourite at Pompey in a sort of ner, ner ner ner ner ner ner, ner ner ner ner ner ner" format– but felt that this might detract from the enjoyment of their evening. They escaped the madness at Farncombe and I was glad that I hadn't spoiled the occasion for them.

It occurred to me, on the journey from Farncombe to Petersfield how odd it is that such a working class game can produce songs adapted from opera. In addition to the above, what about La Donna e Mobile, also by Verdi which spawned "Paulo di Canio" or, more familiar to Portsmouth fans, "Dejan Stefanovic". To be effective the chant has to have six syllables which makes it inaccessible to most other than European players. Although it struck me that it would have been suitable for our first goalkeeper Arthur Conan Doyle, if syllables are pushed to the limits.

The train finally crawled into Petersfield at 00.25. We hopped into Paddy's car and sped home at a higher speed than any train we'd sat in all day. The Hyundai was still in the station car park, immaculately parked, but there was no sign of the young oriental man.

Dagenham ranks as the worst away evening I've ever done. The journey up and back had been a nightmare and the football on offer had been possibly the worst I'd seen all season if not in my entire football-watching life. I wouldn't want to deter anyone from going to an away match there but I shall be forever scarred. The only redeeming feature had been the burgers but I could have driven down to Portsdown Hill and bought a Mick's Jaw Breaker for a fraction of the cost of this away experience.

CHAPTER FIVE

NORTHAMPTON

It was only because we'd already pre-booked that we went to Cambridge – see Chapter One. But having won there at a canter, following it up with a string of February 3-pointers, Dagenham was quickly forgotten and we looked at the fixture list to see where we might go next.

We settled on Northampton which was a Tuesday night game in March and just about accessible if Paddy could get off work early. He managed to pull a flanker and we left about 4pm, accompanied by Kieran, with Paddy driving.

For a Portsmouth fan, Northampton is iconic. In the late 70s we were in a very similar position in the old Fourth division. A new manager, Frank Burrows, ex-Swindon and a dour Scottish journey man professional, was appointed manager and he bought some seasoned pros such as Joe Laidlaw, well-known at Middlesbrough but nearing the end of his career, and Terry Brisley, ex-Orient, who became known as "far post Brisley" due to his knack of popping up at the far post to stick home a cross. We had a prolific striker in Colin Garwood who had scored goals throughout the lower divisions. The rest of the team was made up of solid players and we started the season well, but like in 2014/15, went through a spell when we just couldn't muster a point away. From leading the table for a long period we slipped back and come the last game of the season we had to win at Northampton and hope that Bradford didn't get a win at home if we were to secure promotion.

Most of the city went to Northampton. All of my present fellow fans and old school mates made the trip. At the time I was at Poly at Newcastle so planned to join them at the match using a different route. It was all planned down to strategic perfection, the mid –morning train from Newcastle to Birmingham, a connection to Northampton, and a couple of beers before the game. It turned out more like Gallipoli.

Michelle and I went to a house party the night before the game. We had recently got engaged. Having a few sherbets before the party, which was in Jesmond, we went on to the house and I was careful to moderate my consumption out of respect for the following day's necessities. Michelle's dad had been in his younger days a fanatical Newcastle fan but he hadn't instilled the passion for football in any of his three daughters. She just really didn't know what the fuss was about when I was talking about one of the most important games in my lifetime of being a Portsmouth supporter. We got disentangled during the evening and one of my last memories that night was seeing her drinking real ale out of a saucepan. Suffice to say that the following morning she was not in good condition, and after she endured a number of vomiting episodes I was required, looking at my watch all the time, to walk her to her bus stop to catch the bus back to the coast.

I got as fast as I could to Newcastle Central but not in time to catch the train to Birmingham and onwards to The Promised Land. I looked at the timetables and settled upon Peterborough as the next best option. Bear Grylls once again kicking in, I told myself that it was a fast train from Newcastle which would get in at Peterborough about 2 and it would be easy to hitch a lift to Northampton which I figured was about 30 miles away. The first bit was fine, the train was on time and

I emerged at Peterborough confident that I'd make the game. Two hours later, having walked and hitched unsuccessfully for about 8 miles, I'd virtually given up. Then at last something happened which made me realise there really is a God.

A spanking new Daimler stopped, and the driver asked where I wanted to go. I replied that I'd hoped to get to Northampton FC, and explained why. My eternal good fortune was that he was a Northampton Director, who had been delayed but who was popping in for the post match hospitality. He admitted my torn jeans to his passenger seat without requiring me to go through any sort of flea-ridding rigmarole, and despatched me at the back of the away end about 4.30. He will never know how this act of generosity impacted upon me although I thanked him effusively. I just walked through the open gate to the over-capacitied away end to hear that we were a goal up and that Bradford were goalless. Almost immediately we scored a second and the transistor radios were focussed on Valley Parade. When the final whistle blew, there was the typical pitch invasion of the time. Word came through that Bradford had only drawn and the celebrations erupted

I had to get back to Newcastle the following day and made my way across to Bedfordshire to stay overnight with some old family friends. My mates hit London and danced in the Trafalgar Square fountain, apparently much to the amusement of passers-by who had no idea what Portsmouth FC had possibly done to encourage such euphoria.

But back to the present. Northampton now played at the Sixfields Stadium which is quite conveniently on the A43 coming from Oxford. We aimed for the main club car park and were there with about an hour to spare. The ground is on the outskirts of Northampton adjacent to a retail estate and the options for a quick beer and food in any of a selection of pubs are not extensive. We decided to give the bowling alley bar a miss in favour of something more traditional, and eventually got to the top of the hill where we found a pub which I think was called The Rover. Whatever it was called, it sold decent beer and after a couple of pints we made our way down to the ground. Whilst in the garden of the pub, having a smoke, I could see down to the stadium with the floodlights on, and it was a bit like being on Henman Hill at Wimbledon or Trundle Hill at Goodwood racecourse. It was tempting to see if I could stay in the pub for 90 minutes and watch the game from their garden, but I decided not to risk it for a biscuit. Instead we strolled to the away end past numerous burger vans and other mobile food outlets. You won't lack for edible sustenance outside the Sixfields.

Entering the ground it was a cut above most League Two stadiums. Northampton had managed to move from the old ground to something more modern whilst presumably maintaining solvency, something which had eluded us for years. The Sixfields was a work in motion but its infrastructure promised an optimistic future for the supporters even though it was not huge.

The away end was a comfortable option. Not massive but covered. There was a good away contingent but there were still seats to spare. Unfortunately, it proved to be a typical 14/15 Pompey away experience.

We had recently sold our diminutive winger Ricky Holmes to Northampton. Ricky was one of our first signings when we exited administration near the start of our first League Two season. He was short on stature but became popular with Pompey supporters due to an effort level which made up for his technical inadequacies. Sometimes played right midfield and sometimes left side, he promised much but invariably delivered little, particularly when playing on the left and driven wide by defenders. What couldn't be faulted was his work rate and it was this which masked his inadequacies with the fans. If he lost the ball he'd run miles to get it back. I seem to recall that he was voted our player of the year – really only for this reason – in our first season back in League Two, and in fairness, probably deservedly so when compared to his peers.

Ricky emerged in the early 2014/15 season with a little top knot. Now I can understand why Ibrahimovic might just about get away with that, but not in League Two. Wayne Rooney can wear gloves in the Premier League and no-one is going to take liberties with him, but if you wear gloves in anything from about League One down to Portsmouth Sunday League division 7, you are asking for people to kick shit out of you. For this reason I think most fans suddenly saw Ricky as a pretentious pratt. His performances were not cutting edge to boot and he somewhat lost his mojo. He told the local press that he thought his best position was a roving role behind the strikers. Having convinced the manager to play him there once, it was against the most physical team in the division and on the boggiest pitch of that season. It proved to be a disaster and the experiment was never repeated.

Whatever happened, Ricky moved to Northampton in mid-season, I think from most fans perspectives with thanks for the effort he'd put in, but acknowledging that we weren't going to get any more from him. In the month or two since he'd left us he had seemingly single-handedly galvanised Northampton's season to the extent that they had become real play-off contenders, and this from the free role that he had only played once, and dismally, for us.

The teams entered the arena and when the game started Ricky, who thankfully had abandoned his top-knot for a more conventional haircut, began the game well. It was puzzling that players who had presumably witnessed his limited array of tricks in training for the last couple of years, seemed suddenly bewildered by him. We made him look like Cristiano Ronaldo. Whenever he attacked down our left side, our full back Dan Butler backpedalled like an Italian soldier.

Northampton were attacking the away fans end in the first half and it was surprising and somewhat disappointing that he was booed by a large section of our supporters when he got on the ball. He'd not asked for a move and was freely released when Northampton came knocking. He'd never been a free loader when he'd played for us and I'd expected that whilst the Pompey fans would be neutral towards him they wouldn't boo or abuse him. I thought we had a better set of supporters than that.

It was therefore no surprise that when he once again bedazzled Butler and cut inside to plant a curling shot beyond Jones into the corner of our net with his weaker foot, he put his finger to his lips in the Shhh gesture, though at least he ran towards the side terrace where the only remotely vociferous Northampton fans were sitting. The same Pompey fans who'd been booing him seemed the most incensed by this. In fact, Northampton supporters made the Library at Highbury seem like a music festival. There were a couple of blokes in puffa jackets trying to whip up some frenzy, but unsuccessfully, which prompted the mocking chant "two fans, you've only got two fans".

Now call me old–fashioned but I wondered why the same Pompey fans who'd booed Holmes should be offended by his subdued goal celebration. I confess that it winds me up when an innocuous away midfielder, who hasn't had any stick all game, plants one in our net and then runs to the home supporters puffing his chest out and giving it some. OK me old cock, you've just scored in front of the biggest stand in League Two and it's probably the highlight of your career before your contract expires and you end up playing part time at Margate or somewhere, but it's just inflammatory.

It's a lot different if you've been given stick all game. I can remember a couple of players who got abuse, friendly or otherwise, but who seemed to treat it like water off a duck's back. As you'd guess, one was Robbie Savage who seemed to revel in abuse (particularly when sheep were mentioned in the songs) and Gary Neville, whose credentials as an England right back were questioned at about every football ground in the country. Both just seemed to play better when the world was against them. But my favourite example of this was Paul Dickov. He became almost a cult hate figure at Fratton partly because he played for Leicester, one of our biggest bogey teams, but mainly because he was, well, just Paul Dickov.

I remember one particular game when the Pompey Chimes rang out to the refrain of "F... off Dickov, Dickov F...off". He prompted these chants because he was constantly around the referee whingeing how he'd not got a free kick or a corner. I remember at a corner he stood on the near post, hampering our keeper and giving a few elbows. The torrent of abuse would have made Frankie Boyle blush, but he just smirked at the crowd and played to the abuse. A couple of minutes later he scored. Frankly, I would have said good on you if he'd given it some, but he just celebrated with team mates and gave us a little wave. Much as I hated the short-arsed Scots git, I could live with that.

But I digress yet again. Half-time came soon afterwards, and we discussed our chances of recovering something from the game. We weren't optimistic, even though we'd probably shared first half possession. The fact was that if we lost this one, our charge to the play-off spots would have finally fizzled out.

We came out with slightly renewed vigour after half-time and were the better team in the second half, but apart from a couple of decent saves by the Northampton keeper we never really looked destined to take the three points, let alone one.

About 10 minutes from the end of the game, Northampton substituted Ricky. Now this is one of football's more puzzling statistics. In fact I'm not aware that there are any statistics but I'm sure if Statto got his head down on this one he would prove me right. Why is it that when a team is winning and makes a late substitution, the player being substituted is always on the far side of the pitch from the dugout? They then stroll across the pitch about the speed of Neil Armstrong walking on the moon. They will stop in the centre circle and do a twirl around the centre spot clapping the fans. The referee, realising that he is supposed to add 30 seconds for a substitution and this one's already taken two minutes with the player only halfway across the pitch, will run across and pat him on the arm to hurry up, which the player will promptly ignore. And at the end of the game, when the referee adds on just 3 minutes when there have been at least 10 minutes spent on getting players off the pitch, the ref will wonder why fans start howling. So here are my rules for substituted players:-

1. Get your arse off the pitch quick.
2. No stopping to clap the fans on the way off. Especially if they are like Northampton's fans emerging from slumber.
3. If, on the contrary your fans have been as noisy as say Stoke or Crystal Palace, you are permitted to clap but only while still moving. And without a pirouette in the centre circle. Further, you must clap in a masculine way which means hands above your head and full-blooded. None of this effeminate polite clapping at the side of your body. It just looks like you're in the parlour clapping an Elizabeth Bennett piano recital from Pride and Prejudice.
4. A note to referees; yellow cards if they don't get off the pitch quickly. I pay good money to watch football and want a full 90 minutes. This must rankle even more if you're paying Stamford Bridge prices.

Naturally, apart from the effeminate clapping which is a non-starter anywhere, these rules do not apply to Pompey players when we're winning.

Having witnessed Ricky take an interminable exit, we pressed forward again and exerted some real pressure. The referee added on 4 minutes and we were camped in their half. The ball was cleared and our captain on the night Ben Chorley, who was already on a yellow card, went up for a challenge which looked innocuous enough but resulted in another yellow. Now most people, even footballers with an IQ less than zero, would realise that at 1-0 down and 4 minutes left on the clock, argument, which is fruitless anyway, is also self-defeating to your team and your supporters. Not Ben. He proceeded to spend half of the added time arguing about the decision. It was only when he seemingly heard the collective howls of "get off the pitch, you wanker", from his own team's fans, that the penny finally dropped and he made his exit. He was released at the end of the season, and I don't know where he's playing now, but don't expect to see him turning up on Mastermind.

Any momentum lost, the game drifted to another defeat and our 2014/15 season was effectively over. It was the last away journey we were tempted to make though Paddy did take the long trip to Carlisle a few weeks later, primarily prompted by a greater desire for a night out across in Newcastle after the game.

A midweek game is always a depressing experience. It's work the following day and even if the journey is short, you are always going to be late hitting the sack. It seemed that tonight would be later than we hoped because we'd parked in the club car park and it must have taken 30 minutes to get out. However Paddy got so much out of his 1.2 Ford Fiesta that we raced down the M1, round the M25 and down the A3 in just under two hours. The engine was strained to the limit and I reckoned that if he'd floored the accelerator any more we would have ended up like the Anthill mob from Wacky races. They reckon a good jockey gets the best out of every horse he rides. On this performance in motoring terms I'd trust Paddy with a Fiat 500.

So it was goodbye and good riddance, apart from Cambridge, to season 2014/15 away days. I wondered what would be in store the following year.

CHAPTER 6

A NEW SEASON

Season 2014/15 ended like a damp squib. Our remote chance of making the play-offs ended with Northampton and a few games later Andy Awford was relieved of his managerial duties. His last hurrah had been February when he had been voted the League Two manager of the month, but the quality of the opposition that month had always suggested that with even a modicum of improvement we were likely to pick up a few points. With a couple of subsequent injuries to key players revealing the lack of quality in their replacements, and some disappointing performances both at home and away, it was only a matter of time before an agreement was reached to part by mutual consent. It was unfortunate that his early promise as a manager was not enduring but amongst the fans there was some confusion as to what he thought was his best formation and endless tinkering, which would have made Claudio Ranieri's teams look models of stability, meant that players often looked uncomfortable in the formations or in the specific position they were being asked to play. I think many fans were sad to see him leave but even his most diehard supporters were forced to concede that we didn't appear to have shown real signs of upward progress over his tenure. His replacement Gary Waddock was only ever going to have a temporary caretaker's role but as Andy's assistant manager over a run of poor results he was always likely to be tainted with the same brush and never really to be considered a permanent solution. Results through to the end of the season were in and out and we finished well clear of the relegation spots but in a lowly 17th position, the worst in our modern history.

The parting of the ways with Andy before the end of the season gave the Board some breathing space to consider his replacement. They obviously received a number of applications from established managers with proven track records, and some with mixed past fortunes. The local rag put a different name in the frame virtually every day, but gradually it emerged that the man they wanted was Paul Cook the current Chesterfield manager. As supporters we will never know if he applied for the job or was targeted, or a bit of both, but he was under contract to Chesterfield and they stonewalled the approach as you might expect.

Chesterfield had left League Two a year earlier but most fans could remember them as a footballing side with an unusually patient footballing ethos. We had not seen much of the ball in our home game against them but they had not seemed unduly ambitious to go for the win even after we had a player sent off at the end of the first half. In the end they sneaked a late winner. I can't even remember how we ended up against them on their manor but clearly Cook had built a decent side on a fairly modest budget and they were eventually promoted automatically as champions, also getting to the final of the paint pot trophy.

In the season just past they had threatened to make it two in a row with a further promotion but eventually finished in the play-off spots. The first of the two legged semi was due to be played when our interest became known and I felt a little sorry for them that their team must have been unsettled by possible changes in the near future. They lost convincingly over two legs to Preston, and Chesterfield eventually bowed to the inevitable and agreed to the release of Cook on payment of £150,000 compensation or so it was reported.

Paul Cook soon made his mark. He appeared to have already formed the view that a complete clear out was necessary in a club which had underperformed woefully, given its fan base and potential income, over the previous two years. Virtually everyone who was out of contract was released. A couple of those names were a little surprising but the supporters were desperate to place trust in someone who had proved himself successful at this level and there was little dissent. It was interesting that the majority of the released players seemed to start the summer on trials with similar level clubs but gradually dropped their sights to non-League football. If nothing else this was a good indicator to the fan base that most had not really been up to scratch at this level and the new manager had been correct in being brutal with his purge.

There were a couple of other notable departures. Inevitably, having failed to secure promotion with Pompey, Jed Wallace finally succumbed to the attentions of Wolves who paid the release clause in his contract. Admittedly this was not a true reflection of his real worth, certainly to us, but the low release figure had clearly given him the confidence to sign up a new contract, and who knows where we might have finished without his performances and goal tally the previous season. Virtually without exception Pompey fans seemed resigned to his departure and hoped that he'd go on to have a successful career elsewhere.

Another departure, by consent, was Johnny Ertl, an Austrian, who had a year left on his contract. Johnny was no Messi but he always gave his all for us and although some supporters were very disparaging of his skill levels, others recognised his commitment and also noted that sometimes if he was substituted, holes appeared in our defensive midfield.

He had also formed an affection for the club and the city; in some ways on a different level he was a little like one of our early 21st century overseas favourites, Arjan de Zeeuw. When Johnny's departure was publicised there were few who wished him ill, even amongst his biggest critics. He was later elected as a member of the board of the Supporters Trust

Of the existing squad the remainder who were under contract were retained but one suspected that a number were told their fortune, and some voluntarily moved on to new clubs. The most surprising was Paul Robinson who was one of our best players in the previous season; his departure to Wimbledon was the first decision which Paul Cook had made to which some cracks of dissent amongst the fans were apparent. Seemingly however Robbo had the opportunity to extend his career elsewhere and being given a blunt indication that he could not be guaranteed a starting place every week, flipped a coin and decided to move. It looked to be that there had been a refreshing honesty about the player's approach to the manager and the manager's response to the player and again, no-one could really be easily wound up by either. Robbo was very solid as a defender but not known for his silky passing skills out of defence and it seemed that the manager was looking for players comfortable on the ball in every position. Again, he went with a lot of support.

The only player out of contract who was retained was Adam Webster. He'd been played at right back when he got a game under Andy Awford, and had looked uncomfortable, but when moved by Waddock to his preferred centre half position at the end of the last season he had looked competent if at times a little lightweight against bulky target men. He had shown excellent distribution from the back and it was probably this which persuaded our new manager to retain him.

We had a few other promising youngsters in Conor Chaplin, a diminutive striker with good positional skills and clever on the ball, and Ben Close, a holding midfielder. Together with a left back promoted from the youth team, Brandon Haunstrup, they looked set to become part of the squad. Jack Whatmough had already become established as a first team regular, but had suffered an injury which was likely to keep him out until Christmas.

Which left our keeper Paul Jones, Nigel Atangana, Danny Hollands, James Dunn, and Matt Tubbs. Jones had been an ever present in the previous year. Competent on crosses, and having blocked many point blank efforts, his weakness appeared to be that he was caught out perhaps more than he should have been on longer range efforts. On the eve of the season a new keeper, Brian Murphy, was signed on loan from QPR and he surprisingly got the nod for the first league game of the season.

Nigel Atangana had been signed from local non-league club Havant and Waterlooville for a small fee. Andy Awford clearly however didn't fancy him in a 4-4-2 formation and his chances to impress had been limited, never getting a run in the side. Early on in 2014/15 he had looked like a real footballer with incisive passing skills and it became apparent after the early season 2015/16 friendlies that his new manager rated him.

Nigel had been kept out of the side by Danny Hollands who had been signed on an extensive contract having helped sparked our end of season flurry of points while on loan in 2013/14. He had failed to sparkle at all however after he'd signed a 3 year contract and looked a shadow of his earlier self in the 2014/15 season.

James Dunn had been our most combative midfielder in 14/15 and we had clearly missed him when he was out injured for a couple of months that autumn. However it soon became apparent that his long daily commute from Kent was not seen by the manager as conducive to high performance or commitment to the club, and at the start of the 2015/16 season, it looked unlikely that he would feature prominently. Most fans felt that he would not struggle to find another club nearer to his home, and that an extended loan or transfer at some stage would be likely.

Which left Matt Tubbs. Top scorer and voted League Two player of the year, it seemed inconceivable that he would not form a central part of the new manager's plans.

However the squad had been thinned down massively, and the cull had seemed pretty brutal. We just hoped that the replacements would be of better quality. Over the last couple of seasons on the whole we had been restricted to some extent by our former emergence from legal administration, and incoming players rarely seemed to be of any higher standard than those they replaced. However, we had now paid off all our debts, and sold more season tickets than the year before. This coupled with Paul Cook's preference for working with a smaller more stable squad, meant that we were able to attract better quality players with experience of playing in the leagues above.

One early signing was Gary Roberts who arrived from the manager's former club, Chesterfield. He had a good reputation as a top class creative midfield player at this level. Other arrivals were Kyle Bennett from Doncaster, another forward midfielder or wide player, and Kal Naismith from Accrington, a Scot who had previously been at Rangers, and also a wide midfielder. To complete the midfield acquisitions, Michael Doyle signed from Sheffield United, an experienced defensive midfield player and Gareth Evans arrived from Fleetwood, a more offensive wide player who had scored a fair goals to games ration in League One.

We seemed to be awash with midfield players but perhaps unsurprisingly in view of the new Manager's preferred 4-2-3-1 formation. We wondered where the defenders were coming from but the signing of Christian Burgess a monstrously tall central defender from Peterborough, and a young loanee from Ipswich, Matt Clarke, provided some re-assurance. The left back spot was clearly earmarked for Enda Stevens who had also been at Doncaster the previous season.

The spot which took longest to fill was at right back but after a few triallist friendlies, Ben Davies, a right sided utility player, signed from Sheffield Utd. There was one final, possibly speculative addition in Ben Tollitt who had been plying his wares in non-league football with Skelmersdale. For the start of the season at least, the squad was now complete.

The fixture list was eagerly awaited. From the perspective of green miles, the season would be better with Barnet and Bristol Rovers promoted at the expense of Cheltenham and more particularly Tranmere. Relegated to our division were Notts County, Crawley, Leyton Orient and Yeovil. We had lost, to promotion, Bury, Burton Albion, Shrewsbury and Southend. Road trips looked shorter.

When the fixture list was released I was keen to work out where I'd explore in the coming season. I highlighted places, or grounds, that I'd not visited before, and put on the back burner those I'd already done, unless of course it was an end of season game which might mean automatic promotion or a route to the play offs.

The first game was at home and away games in August would be Plymouth, Crawley and Luton. I had been to Plymouth before – many years ago when we had won the then division 3 championship. It was a fair old trek and I decided against. It did however remind me of my days at University in Newcastle when I realised that much as southerners were ridiculed for having no understanding of geography north of Watford, the Northerners were no better. My Geordie mates would describe Portsmouth v Plymouth as a local derby and I'd put them right by replying "Yeah, if you consider Newcastle v Notts Forest to be a local derby". Dockyard Derby yes, local derby no.

I'd also been to Kenilworth Road before and Luton is in my opinion such a complete dump that I had no inherent desire to visit again. In my old Dad's Hampshire burr, it's a"pergy hole". In any event, the day of the Luton game was my wedding anniversary and something had to give if I was going to be trolling all over the country at weekends for the next 9 months. I booked an overnight stay in Maidenhead and a hospitality package at Royal Windsor racecourse ladies day instead. That ought to be worth a couple of months brownie points. Windsor is a cracking little racecourse track particularly on a balmy summer evening, when you can take a riverboat from Windsor centre right to the racecourse itself. It's well worth a visit.

The Crawley game was on a Tuesday night. I'd not been to their ground before so that had to be the first on the list.

We started the season well. A 3-0 home win against a poor Dagenham side gave us optimism and when we played virtually a second string in the Capital One cup against Derby and won deservedly, playing decent football in the process, the optimism increased. When our second league game at Plymouth resulted in a 2-1 win against a team with a traditionally good home record, expectations went off the Richter scale. Would this be the season which turned round our recent fortunes? I'd get my first away view of the team at Crawley.

CHAPTER 7

CRAWLEY

It had been a typical English summer. The clouds had come in on virtually every day which had started cloudless. It took until June before I was able to fire up the barbeque and even then we ate indoors. Balmy evenings sitting in the garden proved non-existent and the football season had crept up unnoticed.

The website advertised tickets for the Crawley away game in the second week of August. I'd gauged interest and Chop and Steve immediately put their names in the frame. Andy, being married to a teacher at a local primary school, was forced to take his holidays in peak season and was going to be basting himself in Cyprus. He described his holiday as if he was a member of the SAS, braving the far east of the Med and its proximity to Syria, and the base for military action in the region. If he wasn't half Greek it would be easy to believe him.

The ticket office hotline opened at 9 a.m on a Monday. I figured that it would be popular being, albeit a Tuesday night game, easily accessible from Portsmouth. In off peak hours I could get to Gatwick in 55 minutes from my home a little up the A3 so it was one of those occasions when you could leave work on time and still make an away game. I hung on the line listening to some inane music and receiving frequent apologies every 30 seconds, but eventually, after about 20 minutes, I got through to order 3 seats. Crawley was one of those venues where you could choose to stand or sit but we decided that our knees being what they were we would go for the seated option. I succeeded in getting seats but resolved to ring up BT to register the Pompey ticket office one of my friends and family options for the future.

I had reduced my working hours to three days a week and took Monday and Tuesday off. Steve had himself decided to retire completely so Chop was the only one of us at work on a Tuesday.

We had a long and fruitless e-mail exchange about how we'd get there and who would be driving. We all stuck our hands up for this task. I'm happy to drive, no I'm happy to drive, I don't mind driving; or shall we hop on a train? After several rounds of "I'm Spartacus, no I'm Spartacus" we eventually resolved the issue in our regular half-time dissection of the performance at our home game against Dagenham in the Fratton end concourse the Saturday before. We concluded that we weren't going anywhere until Chop had finished work and got to us, so it was logical that he would drive. He decided the best route would be up the A3, along the A272, and up the A23. I was on the way so we'd meet up at my house whenever he could get there after work.

My long weekends had turned into a bit of a routine. I'd do all my regular jobs on a Saturday morning. Food shop in and grass cut it would be a sandwich and off to the match or maybe an afternoon on the sofa watching Soccer Saturday and that consummate presenter Jeff Stelling. There is always at least one quip which prompts a laugh, and on the afternoon of couch potatoing for the Plymouth away game it was "Allo allo allo, James Constable has just scored for Eastleigh."

Sundays are generally fairly lazy, maybe doing the competition at our golf club, and watching football in the afternoon; if I don't play golf on Sunday, we'll get a group together and play at another course on Monday. Which leaves Tuesdays for taking the dog for a walk on the downs, coming home and going straight out for lunch somewhere.

Chop worked in Southampton for his sins. I'd have to wear a string of garlic pearls if I worked in a SO postcode, he satisfied himself with wearing his Pompey club tie. He reckoned if he got away at 5 he could get to my house about 6. Plenty of time for me to indulge my usual Tuesday routine. Michelle and I took the dog for a decent walk, and got in the car over to the Red Lion at Chalton where a nice bit of pork fillet and a slice of black cherry cheesecake put me in sleep mode for the afternoon. I managed to drop off for an hour to the backdrop of A Place in the Sun, and woke up in time to pick Steve up from town and bring him back out ready for Chop's arrival. As it happened, school holidays meant that Chop made good time and we were on the road from my place before 6.

Now Chop has a Smart car. It's the 4 seater variety but still fairly squat. He bought it mainly because parking in Pompey is a real trial but he has a front garden which he converted into a hardstanding. Even then the garden wouldn't accommodate anything sizeable so he went for a Smart car. When we got in the car he apologised in advance for the fact that at speed the vehicle would make a lot of noise if he put his foot to the floor. Being pretty deaf and unable to hold a conversation in a car at the best of times, I suggested that I sit in the back so that Steve could chat in the front. Occasionally they would ask (shout) me a question which they usually had to repeat three times before they got an answer, and even then in the majority of cases the answer bore no relation to the question.

We bombed up the A3 for 10 minutes before joining the A272 at Petersfield. The A272 is a very pretty road which runs from Winchester in Hampshire along the South Downs to Uckfield in East Sussex. Along the way it offers great views of the South Downs and passes through several pretty villages. Its' appeal is such that a Dutchman (at least, I think he was a Dutchman) called Pieter Boogaart was so taken with it that he felt compelled to write a book about its attractions. He called the book "an Ode to a Road". I rather liked the fact that someone could be so taken with a stretch of tarmac that he would write a book about it but then again I suppose that you could say that about anything, including football awaydays. Only at lunchtime, whilst there had been a lull in our conversation at the Red Lion, had I spotted on a bookshelf a book about three inches thick devoted entirely to an encyclopaedia of roses. I have the utmost admiration for anyone who has the patience and dedication to put together a compendium of this magnitude, so perhaps I shouldn't be surprised about the Dutch cyclist's affection for the A272.

There aren't many decent overtaking spots on the A272, so the time in which you can get from A to B is dictated largely by the speed of the other vehicles. So it was an irritation but even more a surprise when on about a 6 mile stretch of twisting road with Trotton at its epicentre we came across a phenomenon which I'd never seen before; a motor cyclist travelling well within the speed limit. I've got nothing against bikers provided they assume when riding their bikes that they are driving a car. By that I mean when I'm on a dual carriageway, overtaking a lorry transporting a mobile home, the bike doesn't decide that it's perfectly safe to squeeze in between us at 120 miles an hour. I get immensely irritated when motorway gantries tell me to "think bike" when so many bikers seem so oblivious to steps they could take to maximise their own safety.

So much as normally I would have had the greatest of respect for a motorcyclist bucking the trend, at 6.25 on a match night with us still 40 miles from our destination it was a somewhat unwelcome law-observance. Fortunately he turned off left and we hit a stretch of straight road where Chop made up the time. We'd passed Harting Down on our right and straddled our way through Midhurst which can so often be a bottleneck, and on to Petworth which has a curious and twisty one-way system running along the walls of Petworth House. Petworth itself is a rather unusual little place, with lots of antique shops complemented by more upmarket looking curry houses and a couple of pubs. As you get to the other side of the town you also go past what I've always described as the Hobbit houses – small terraced cottages with front doors which are about 4 foot high. As we drove past I imagined Bilbo strolling out with Gandalf bent double.

On the stretch of road from Petworth to Billingshurst lies a village called Wisborough Green. It's a place I have always thought that I'd like to live one day. It is a quintessentially English village, a mix of older and more modern houses free of the development which hardly anywhere seems able to escape Government housing quotas. It has a typical village green – they were playing cricket on the evening we passed through – a quaint looking village stores and a pub where you could probably sit over a pint of Badger putting the world to rights with your next-door neighbour for an hour or two. I bet every meal there is served with jus.

As we made our exit from the village we passed, on the left, a house with a most magnificent garden. It wasn't so much that it had a host of bright colour but it was a mass of different shrubs. I'd been passing through Wisborough Green on my way to Gatwick for about 20 years and I don't think the garden has changed much if at all over this period. It struck me that it was virtually maintenance free apart from an annual pruning and I could appreciate the forethought of someone who had probably designed and planted out tiny plants many years ago with the imagination to work out what it might look like 20 or 30 years ahead. I just wished I had the same skill. Every year I say that I am going to design my back garden in a way that offers year round colour and minimal maintenance. But every year I still have the late spring panic that means that I'm off to B and Q for a few trays of petunias and Bizzy Lizzies just to afford the outside of the house a bit of colour.

Which made me think of B and Q. Well you do go from A to B to C to D when you're in the back seat of a car with a screaming engine without any conversation save for the odd question posed through a virtual loudspeaker or in some sort of hybrid sign language. I was reminded of a Pompey chant from the Noughties. The News of the World or a similar rag had reported that our right back Glen Johnson had been arrested for shoplifting a toilet seat from B and Q, or at least changing the price tag to pay less. The first thing that occurred to me was how bizarre it was that a footballer on his sort of wages might even feel the need to do this with anything, let alone a toilet seat from B and Q. The first thought of some wag however was to turn it into a song which surfaced at the following game, to the tune of Winter Wonderland:

"One Glen Johnson
There's only one Glen Johnson
With his toilet seat from B and Q
Johnson is the England number 2"

Glen has of course long moved on to pastures new with Liverpool and was now playing for Stoke. So Stoke fans, feel free to borrow this little ditty. Just substitute "was" for "is" to bring it up to date.

We careered along the road to the A23, catching the lights on green at virtually every main road that dissected the A272, slipped on to the A23 and left at the Crawley exit just after 7pm. Steve had been to Crawley before, so gave the directions. It's only a short distance from the A23 to the ground and it's located in an out of town commercial district so for an evening game it wasn't difficult to park. We had about a quarter mile walk to the ground, so Steve and I decided to take the paved route and via the pedestrian crossing on the dual carriageway, while Chop, who hadn't had the luxury of food before we left, was keen to sample the pies and decided to play chicken amongst cars going at speeds to which his Smart car could only aspire. We slipped through a hedge and arrived at the ground at 7.15, with time for a quick beer before the match. There were no pubs nearby but the Crawley FC bar, titled Redz, was open to home and away fans. There were people drinking inside and outside, it was all pretty cordial, and easy to get served. Chop had a bottle of Becks, Steve a pint of Fosters and I spied a bottled beer in the fridge called 1698 Kentish Ale. It turned out to be one of those beers that says quality rather than quantity. The first couple of sips made me realise this was no ordinary beer and when I checked the ABV on the label it was 6.5%. I'd never seen it before but resolved to check it out further. When I later looked at the website for Shepherd Neame I discovered that they could describe their beer as Kentish Ale, a bit like Parma ham and Champagne, without breaching any pathetic EU directives.

Steve and I took our time over our beer but Chop downed his quickly, keen to get amongst the pies, so went on in to the ground. We followed and settled into our seats in the Checkatrade stadium, as Crawley's ground was embarrassingly named, about 5 minutes later. We were seated in the West stand, half of which was given to home and half to away supporters. It was a nice enough stand by League Two standards. The only bizarre aspect to it was the roof which looked semi-permanent and made of some sort of toughened tarpaulin. I wondered if it was a retractable covering a bit like the roof on Centre Court at Wimbledon but on a lower scale. Probably not because we were in August, it was dry, and there wouldn't be many more chances to retract it over the coming months.

The teams emerged at the halfway line on the opposite side of the ground and we were unchanged from our earlier league matches. To my right and half way across, the Pompey fans manned one and a half ends of terracing. The tallest stand, for the home supporters took up the rest of the length of the pitch on the opposite side, and the end to my left was a small covered terraced end occupied by the Crawley fans.

The Pompey fans on the terraces passed along the crowd the latest flag. I think this was one about "not breaking our spirit". I have to say I'd always thought that this flag was a bit dramatic and corny, even if as supporters we had been through the mill in the last 5 years.

The Crawley supporters at the other end just had a simple banner resting over the hoardings. It said "CTFC Tinpot and proud". That struck me as being a modest but accurate assessment of a team who'd managed to rise from non-League to League One and back down to League Two. Had it not been for the 1700 Pompey fans, the crowd would have been under 2,500. Even the official numbers may have underestimated the away support because it transpired that although officially sold out, a number of Portsmouth fans were told, upon ringing the Crawley ticket office, that they could stand in the away areas as long as they didn't wear colours and were discreet in their support. This seemed an admirable and practical approach and smacked of a club not taking itself too seriously. Unlike the imaginary Howard from Guildford who would probably muse intellectually and self-importantly about segregation on 606, even though he's probably never watched football other than on TV.

We started where we'd left off in previous games, dominating possession. The first 15 minutes passed with Crawley regaining possession for very short periods before we got the ball back again. In League Two terms we looked like Arsenal and they looked like Villa. Except we were the away side and it was Crawley parking the proverbial bus. They had a lone striker Leigh Barnard, who had formerly played at that place along the road and as is customary he was taunted as a "scummer" every time he got near the ball. Which as it happened wasn't very often. There was a gap of about 15 yards between him and his nearest supporting midfielder and he had no chance. If it is ever possible to feel sorry for a scummer I nearly did.

On about 10 minutes Nigel stole the ball in midfield and put a peach of a pass through to Matt Tubbs but he hadn't yet found last season's sharpness and the keeper blocked his shot. Steve and I started to get worried for two reasons. First, we had all the play but hadn't scored. Second, we were 15 minutes into the game and Chop still hadn't found his way to his seat. Whilst we had just the one further chance in the half, when our centre back Matt Clarke really should have buried a free header from a corner, Chop did eventually emerge from Mrs Miggins foodstand in the corner having eaten all the pies. Just one in fact, a chicken and bacon special which he professed to have been "bloody good". He'd apparently seen all of the first 15 minutes from the corner where he'd been left alone by the stewards while he finished off this culinary masterpiece.

The second half saw Pompey attacking our end. It was most notable for our continuing domination of possession and the increasing influence of the linesman immediately in front of us. He looked about 60, although he was probably only 45 and like most linesmen, was profusely balding. Crawley came out playing a high line and a dangerous offside game, but too often we were getting caught. The lineo had his arm in the air more often in one half than the whole 1990s Arsenal back four of Dixon, Adams, Keown and Winterburn managed in a season, and that is saying something. The annoying thing was that every time he got the decision right, except on one occasion when Nigel slipped a short pass through to Matt

Tubbs who coolly clipped the ball over the advancing keeper to make it 1-0. Not according to baldy though who was standing officiously in front of us with his flag in the air. I'd been about level with Tubbs as the pass was put through and was convinced that he was half a yard onside, a view that was clearly shared by the fans around me. A look at the Sky Sports highlights the following day showed that we were correct.

What had been a resigned acceptance of a smarty pants linesman getting everything right now turned into a concerted barricade of abuse whether he got a decision right (most of the time) or wrong (never, apart from the disallowed goal).

One supporter offered the suggestion that he deposit his said flagstick into his rectal orifice, whilst another more colloquially told him to stick his flag "up his Jacksy". A third supporter, in what I felt was an act of kindness and generosity, even pledged to assist him in this process if the flag went up one more time.

I'm not sure what lower league linesmen get paid but I for one would want to be paid a lot to put up with the sort of abuse that baldy received. The difference at lower league level is that you can hear every comment. At Stamford Bridge where let's face it they whinge and whine about everything, the individual comments are lost amongst the moaning of the collective 40,000 when a decision is made that they don't like.

Personally, when my boys played junior football, I hated running the line. Not that I thought I got too much wrong, just that opposing supporters/parents were constantly on your back and you never really got to enjoy watching your own kid play. In Paddy's junior side there had been only a couple of dads who'd played football at any reasonable standard and we were invariably given the flag, but one day we rebelled and the flag was given to Richard, a South African who was a rugby rather than football fan. Richard was a cracking drinking companion on one of those Butlins football tours that most dads have been on with their sons. But he really knew squat about the football offside rule.

So the game started and Richard applied the rugby offside rule to football. Every time the ball was kicked forward, if there was an attacking player in front of the kid who'd kicked the ball, the flag went up, even if there were about 8 defenders between recipient and goal. The howls from the opposing team's parents got louder and louder. It was hilarious and Paul, the other regular linesman, and I figured out immediately what was happening. But Richard was undeterred, until half-time at least when he was given a rundown of the football offside rule and passed the salt and pepper cellar test for the second half. Or alternatively the referee just ignored him completely.

But back to Crawley. Despite severe pressure and almost total possession, we were unable to break them down and the game finished at 0-0, the final whistle bringing a standing ovation from the home fans for their team who'd repelled more assaults than they had at Rorke's Drift. It was a frustrating night for us but I suspected that there would be a few more 0-0s before the season was finished.

We strolled back to the car and discussed the game on the way. It was my last chance to engage in conversation before the car ignition fired, and I was exuding over our retention of possession. Steve was bit less enthused at our inability to penetrate and Chop at one stage confessed that he wasn't a great lover of tippy-tappy football but we all agreed that the fare had been a great improvement on last year's efforts.

So what did I think of the Checkatrade stadium? I decided on the following scores:-

Reliability and timekeeping – 9 – we arrived with time to spare, the game started on time and the referee added on the appropriate minutes to reflect the sluggish substitutions.

Tidiness – 7 – there were plastic glasses everywhere outside Redz bar although in fairness they'd been cleared by the end of the game

Courtesy – 8 – thanks for letting us drink 1698 in your bar and the stewards were OK

Workmanship – 6 – please don't park a bus the next time we play you.

So overall an 8.5 I think but we'll call it a 9 because the 1698 has the casting vote.

We got away from our parking spot reasonably quickly. Chop asked which would be the quickest way back to my house and I reckoned that at this time of night we should go up and round the M25 and down the A3. We'd no sooner joined the M23 than the first motorway gantry flashed up that the M25 junction 10 exit was closed.

Most of the time the information on motorway gantries winds me up a treat. When I'm driving up to visit the in-laws in Durham, and I see that the A1 is closed after the A165891, it sends me in to a blind panic. I have no idea where the A165891 might be and Michelle can't locate it in the atlas, so I have to turn into the next service station to conduct a detailed examination of the map to make sure that I don't have to divert onto the A157614. Invariably I lose half an hour in the process because not only will I discover that the A165891 is about 5 miles short of Edinburgh and thus completely irrelevant to my journey, but Michelle will take the opportunity to visit the loo again, even though she visited the one at the last service station about 20 minutes earlier.

Why can't they say A1 closed near Edinburgh? Or when I'm on the A27 going east that the Brighton turn-off is closed rather than the A-whatever? I really don't think it's helpful when I'm travelling down to the west country if I come out in a cold sweat at the B – something being closed after the A-something only to arrive safely at my destination and examine the atlas (just for the record) to establish that the

B-something was actually somewhere near Grimsby. Why should travel be such an unnecessary stressful experience?

And that's not all while I'm on this subject. I've already ranted that "think bike" should be "think car" but the other one that winds me up is "debris in road". I once hit a temporary 40 limit on the M27 on my way home from a presentation in Southampton at about 10 o'clock at night, coupled with the "debris in road" sign flashing away. Even though I was just about the only car on the road I slowed my speed expecting to see the contents of Steptoe's scrap yard blocking a lane. I travelled about 15 miles before the speed limit reverted to normal and in that time all I saw was a Tesco carrier bag floating around in the middle lane. If you're going to give us these warnings at least update them when you go off for a 3-hour tea break.

And what about "workforce in road"? Why are they there and what the hell are they doing? Perhaps you should talk to them rather than warn me to look out for them. From what I see they put out cones at 10 o'clock at night and pick them up again about 6 in the morning. I have no idea what they do in between.

But on this one, just this one, occasion, the information was helpful. We'd gone up and down the A3 to the M25 enough times to know that J10 is the Guildford/Portsmouth exit, so we pulled off at the next exit, turned round to go back south on the M23, and re-joined the A272, which seems to twist and turn even more in the dark. Steve put on the Best of The Kinks as a sop to the bloke in the back of the car who was not going to have his share of the conversation. The absence of conversation also enabled bloke in back to enjoy a couple of short nodding off episodes whilst Chop threw his Smart car along the A272 in a time which would have made him Test Track champ on Top Gear. We arrived at my house just as "Sunny Afternoon" was ending at about 11.15, long before I was due to turn into a pumpkin.

CHAPTER 8

OXFORD

This could be the shortest chapter of this book. The reason is because Oxford is just about the most dull place to take in an away match.

I'd looked at the fixture list for September and decided that both Oxford and Bristol Rovers were possible. I'd been to away matches at both before, but some years earlier when Oxford played at the Manor Ground and Bristol Rovers at the Eastville Stadium. I'd not been to either of their current stadia.

Since the game against Crawley we had been narrowly knocked out of the league Cup by Reading and out of the paint pot trophy by Exeter, though in the latter we'd put out a side of lads who had barely started shaving and still believed in Father Christmas. It had enabled us to concentrate on the league and we'd had an exciting 3-3 home draw against Morecambe, a good 2-1 away win against highly-fancied Luton at the Pergy Hole, an apparently uninspiring 0-0 draw at home to Accrington and an apparently more inspiring 3-1 home win against Barnet. I say apparently because I was on holiday for both of these home games and had to follow the afternoon's events from a bar in Spain watching Soccer Saturday accompanied by no-one other than my best friend San Miguel.

The Morecambe game had been particularly exciting. 3-0 down and looking as fragile as a Zsa Zsa Gabor marriage, we clawed one back before half-time, got another on the hour, but then had our left back Enda Stevens sent off for a second yellow (justifiably). Two things then happened. Firstly, our passing game seemed completely unaffected by the loss of a man and we continued to dominate patient possession. Secondly, for once a referee recognised incessant time wasting by adding on 6 minutes of added time, in the last of which Jayden Stockley powered a header in off the bar to secure a point. We came away thinking that was what football should be about.

Being away for a week in early September posed logistical problems. Both Oxford and Bristol Rovers tickets went on sale to season ticket holders while I was away. After a round of e-mails it was apparent that Steve was the only one who fancied Oxford. Fortunately he lives less than a mile from Fratton Park and was there bright and early on the Monday to bag our tickets. (He also, bless him, got us Bristol tickets a week later even though he couldn't make that game himself)

I had originally looked at the possibility of doing an overnight at Oxford. Having previously only spent half a day there on a couple of occasions, I rather wanted to explore the city a little more, particularly its University sector. Specifically I wanted to have a good nose around the Bodleian library. I know it seems mutually exclusive to want to couple a League Two football match with a highbrow tour round something as cultural, but I'm a sucker for that sort of stuff. Art leaves me completely cold but give me sight of a Thomas Hardy First Edition or The Magna Carta and I feel like I'm in an Orgasmatron.

I went on Laterooms and started to break out in a cold sweat. Most rooms were over £200 for each of the Friday and

Saturday night. Even those rat-infested hovels with minus stars on Trip Advisor were retailing at over £80 a night. At first I was puzzled why it was all so highly-priced. Then I twigged. It was mid-September and the hotels would be full of the parents of hordes of Crispins and Cressidas starting at the University, probably half of whom would later be sent down in disgrace after running amok with the Bullingdon Club or jumping off bridges into the river in only bras and thongs.

Anyway, the overnight was soon knocked on the head and we decided to go up and back on the same day. Oxford was only an hour and a half from my house and Steve picked me up about 11.30. On this occasion I sat in the front seat and moved my hearing aid from my left to my right ear so I could hear properly, but I suspect that even then my answers and observations strayed into areas which caused Steve to reflect upon whether he'd asked a completely different question than he thought.

"Straight up the A3?"

"I'm happy to stop for a coffee but shouldn't we at least wait till we're on the A34"

"Wonder if it'll be a full house?"

"Yes, painted the hallway last week"

"We're making good time"

"Twelve fifteen according to my watch but I could be a couple of minutes slow."

"You think we'll win today?"

"Really? I thought it had more of an autumnal feel about it."

And so on.

It was probably even tougher for Steve to engage in this conversation because he is one of the most intelligent blokes I knew. He was always the first one you'd ring if you wanted someone for a quiz team. Like his general knowledge, his football knowledge was exceptional. Steve had spent his entire working career in public service, variously as a manager in the job centre or one of the benefit offices.

A number of people I knew had taken this career path. When I came back from university, I played in a Sunday league team over half of which was made up of guys who worked in the Benefits office, and our manager – also our regular linesman – worked there too. I remember with some amusement a Challenge Cup semi against a team from Portsea which contained a centre forward who for the sake of complete anonymity I'll call Peregrine. Peregrine had once been a junior at Pompey but 10 years on and his midriff reflecting a healthy beer intake he was turning out in the Dockyard Premier League. For a bloke his size he was still a good player, mind, but wasn't the brightest. He repeatedly made runs and we just stepped up and caught him offside. After the flag went up for about the twentieth time, Peregine's frustration got the better of him. He shouted over to our linesman "Yeah, you ain't so fuckin' quick with my Giro on Thursdays".

Steve had been to the Kassam Stadium before so knew the ropes. He reckoned that there really wasn't much alternative to parking in the car park immediately surrounding the ground itself. The Kassam is one of those new grounds which has been built somewhat out of town. Looking at the map it's about 5 miles outside Oxford and a bit like Crawley, somewhat in the middle of nowhere. We discussed the option of parking a mile or so away and hoping to get in what was about the nearest pub to the ground, but decided that the likelihood of entry being afforded to Pompey fans, our tickets having sold out, was about as likely as the Green Party winning the next general election.

And so we made straight for the car park, arriving about one o'clock. There must have been space for three or four hundred cars at least but it was already close to full and we ended up in the overflow behind the Oxford home stand.

We walked through the car park observing people reading the morning papers while they waited for the turnstiles to open.

There were two possibilities outside the ground for eats and drinks. One was Frankie and Bennies but neither of us were up for the full sit down experience. The other was the Bowlplex next door. Opting to give it a try, we entered to find that at least it had a big screen showing the lunchtime kick-off which was Chelsea v Arsenal. We eyed the bar and the coffee counter and the queue at both was as long as a queue at an East German bakers in the 1970s, so we decided to stay thirsty until half-time in the TV match and hope that the turnstiles were by then open.

This was the game in which Diego Costa scratched at Koscielny's face. What is it with Suarez's biting and Costa's scratching that our top-flight footballers behave like they're having a fight in the girl's playground? When Gabriel got involved it begged another question. Why cannot someone on such a huge income not show some discipline in the face of provocation, just for 90 minutes? Gabriel was given a red card for a sly, gentle kick. Costa was subsequently banned for three games as well. It demonstrated why most neutral football supporters struggle to like Chelsea. They just ain't got no class, mush. The referee didn't cover himself in glory either. Mike Dean – looks like Jasper Carrott and referees like Jasper Carrott.

Bored through to half-time we left Bowlplex and the unfortunate parents who'd arranged their kids' birthday parties for this particular Saturday. Walking the short distance to the ground we compared what we'd just seen to the Rugby World Cup game between England and Fiji the previous evening. The contrast in discipline and behaviour was marked. Like I've heard many people disillusioned with the Premier League say – "love the game, don't love the players or the Premier League".

Having emerged from Bowlplex, still the turnstiles weren't

open. Steve did a bit of trigonometry and decided that the sun was likely to be in his eyes so we strolled back to his car so that he could get his prescription sunglasses.

There was quite a significant police presence both before and after the game, with a fair smattering of stewards as well. Something was bugging me about the array of police but I couldn't immediately put my finger on it. Eventually I realised why. I only saw one woman. Now at Fratton Park on matchday the sight of a male and female police officer cycling along Goldsmith Avenue in pairs is a familiar sight. Not at Oxford where the policing was almost entirely male.

Now here is a question for the politically correct amongst you. Is it PC for a female police constable to be highlighted as a WPC rather than a PC? Or is it not really PC for a WPC to be so distinguished. Surely it's more PC for a WPC to be PC rather than WPC. You don't see a female Detective Police Superintendent known as WDCS; she's simply a DCS. That's PC. So why not be PC with a PC and a WPC? Strikes me that there's an element of rank distinction at work here.

And here's another thing which strikes me as odd in one of the most PC institutions in the country. I'm talking about the hats. If everyone is supposed to be treated equally, why is it that a male PC gets to wear a helmet or one of the Z car caps but you don't see a woman officer wearing either. No, They wear those sort of stylish trilby ice cream hats. Why is this? I've concluded that unless they crop their hair, it's because they have to wear something like that to accommodate their hairstyles which presumably don't really work with a traditional helmet or a Z cars cap. But let's take this a step further. If Zlatan Ibrahimavitch was to join up with his top knot (or perhaps even Ricky Holmes) he's going to struggle with a helmet or a Z cars cap. A top knot would be ideally suited to one of the ice cream hats that the women wear, but I bet Zlatan and Ricky wouldn't be allowed to wear one.

I think it's just a bit too PC in favour of the WPC.

The ground eventually opened up. I did wonder with so many people sat in cars and sitting on grass banks outside the ground that they have a captive audience at Oxford and why not open the turnstiles early so that people buy more food and drink, but I guess they've done their sums and have worked out that paying staff to work longer isn't balanced by extra sales.

I'm one of those people who can't drink beer after food. Steve on the contrary was hungry so he surveyed the enticing menu. I asked him what he wanted and he was clearly agonising over the decision. It was like Mavis in Coronation Street saying "Ooh I don't know Rita, I just don't know". Eventually though, two criteria were persuasive. First, we saw a bloke eating a burger which looked as appetising as a cowpat. Second, the menu board showed that Oxford sold "award winning pies" by "Chunk". He opted for a cup of coffee and a chicken and mushroom pie. I decided on a can of Marston's Pedigree at an eye-watering £3.80.

Steve's pie was piping hot and like most football ground pies, the bottom could not be extracted from the foil container. Nearly everyone who bought a pie walked away optimistic in their ability to eat it with fingers but as each pie crumbled in their hands they would trot over to collect a plastic fork. I'm a sucker for the chicken tikka pies at Pompey but have only ever once had to eat by hand when they ran out of forks. In the words of my old metalwork teacher it was "entertaining but messy".

Steve finished his pie and stated that he could understand why it was award winning. But as I bought and sunk another can of Pedigree we discussed what awards it might have won. The fact is that you see this everywhere. It's usually award winning ice cream but you never know whether the awards are local or national. Rather sarcastically I suggested that Chunk pies probably won an award as the best pie at the Ottery St Mary district fete. And this is where it all gets a bit spooky. Because when I got home later that day and checked out Chunk pies on the internet it transpires that they are actually based in Ottery St Mary. Their award was for pasties but it was indeed a national award. Perhaps I was being too cynical. I also wondered if I'd lived in Ottery St Mary in a previous life. How else could I have made the connection?

After Steve had talked up the pie, I decided, at about 2.10 pm., that I would have one of their Steak and Kidney variety. Alas, they had sold out. Now I half expect that if I ask for a chicken tikka pie at Portsmouth at 2.45 when there are 18,000 supporters in the ground, I may be disappointed. I don't expect that the steak and kidneys at Oxford, with half that attendance, will sell out by ten past two. I settled for the chicken and mushroom but tried an experiment by letting it cool down a little before I started eating. Result. It came sleekly away from the foil and negated the need for a fork which had anyway sold out with the steak and kidneys. The Pedigree had also sold out so I settled for a coffee.

Steve, who had been put on a Slimming World regime, dutifully rang wife Sue to confess his misadventure with the Chunk pie. I listened on and felt a sense of vicarious guilt.

In the meantime I scoured the concourse and spotted a bloke in what looked like a custom-made hoodie. On the front it just had MUSH in big letters, but there was smaller writing just above. I surreptitiously took my pie receptacle over to the bin next to him just to make out the rest of the words. Immediately above the word MUSH it said "It's a Pompey thing" but he turned away and I couldn't see the rest of what it said.

We made our way to our seats about 2.20. I surveyed the ground. We were at the very top of the away stand, which was shared 50/50 with home supporters though their half was far from full. It was on the side rather than the end of the ground. There is no away end at Oxford.

The stand itself was of a higher quality than most I'd visited. Plenty of leg room and a decent view of the pitch. Lots more rows than at the average League Two ground . Opposite us was a stand of similar proportion with hospitality boxes apparent half way down. It certainly wasn't a flat pack like many newer grounds but was completely let down by the fact that it only had three sides.

The players were out on the pitch, the Pompey players to our right going through a pre-match drill which seemed to involve playing a one-two with the coach and shooting first time at one of those 5-a-side goals specially imported for the practice, guarded by our keeper for the day, on this occasion Paul Jones.

Now here is where I have to mention Barry Harris. Barry has been linked with Pompey since I've been a little boy and he was a grown man. Back in the sixties and seventies when I first went to the ground, Barry was the man who would walk round the pitch on the cinder track between the pitch and the terrace, dressed up in a sailor outfit carrying the placard of the Pompey sailor. The sailor on the placard was smiling, thumbs up for a win. It was replicated in the Football Mail that would be available from about 6.15 in North End. These days, the football pink is an afterthought, something you might pick up on a Sunday morning. In the sixties and early seventies, the Football Mail was blue and you'd hang around outside the newsagents about 6 o'clock, waiting for the van to arrive. The first thing you'd look at was the Pompey sailor in the top corner of the front page. Thumbs up for a win with a smiley face, thumbs down with a grumpy face for a loss and index fingers level for a draw. For away games, all you would know – before you picked up your Football Mail – was the score as read out by James Alexander Gordon on the football pools check at 5 o'clock. You'd know nothing of the detail like the team line-up, who'd scored and when, or who had been sent off, until you got the Football Mail. For a while I seem to remember it was actually delivered on Saturday evening. You'd race to the front door as you heard it pop through the letterbox.

The sailor walking round the pitch had become a bit outdated – or "a bit gay" as modern kids would say. So Barry became a ball boy. At the end of the pre-match kick about he would collect up all the balls in his little net, and at the end of the game he would race on to the pitch to collect the match ball as if he'd personally scored a hat-trick. If we'd won he'd be the last one off the pitch fist-pumping at the Fratton end.

I don't know how old Barry was now but I suspected he'd long ago successfully applied for his bus tokens. So it seemed to me a bit sadistic that as we were engaged in a pre-match warm up next to the fenced end of the Kassam stadium, Barry was stationed in the car park to collect over-hit shots. I watched him for about 15 minutes as balls sailed over the fence. He ran from one end of the car park to the other as balls came flying over, as fast as his hip replacements could carry him. I reckoned we lost at least two balls this day as his back was turned, and by the end of the kick about he must have lost half a stone as he ran around like a kid in the playground. Balls were bouncing off cars as far as Frankie and Bennies. It certainly lightened the boredom as we moved inexorably to kick-off time.

The other thing which was noticeable as the ground filled up was the proliferation of flags. Oxford do love their flags. They pin flags and banners to the back of the home end and gradually as their diehards emerged from the car park, a selection of flags both modest and humungous in size were being waved from the home end. (incidentally, at the end of the game we watched the stewards taking down the fixed banners from the back of the stand, presumably to be recycled at the next home match).

It was nearly kick-off time and I looked up to the sky, expecting the players to arrive not through a tunnel, but by magic carpet, bearing in mind this was after all the Kassam stadium. It was therefore a bit of a let down when they emerged at ground level.

We were missing a key player in Gary Roberts our Mersonesque midfield player, but Conor Chaplin, our local boy, took his place, and he was a competent replacement as far as most were concerned. Otherwise our team looked much the same as it had from the first game. Paul Cook had few Rainieri traits.

Oxford were by now managed by Michael Appleton. He had become Pompey manager shortly before we went in to administration, as a result of which the promised investment opportunities immediately disappeared. As did he after about half a season, escaping the mad house that was Portsmouth for an opportunity at Blackpool, and within two months, he left them to become manager at Blackburn. In short he was a bit of a management slapper. He was sacked by Blackburn after 69 days. I imagine it must have felt like he'd gone out with a couple of ugly women, dumped them both and then himself got dumped by a fit one. Anyway, he had ended up at Oxford.

After a season at Sheffield United, Dave Kitson had signed for Oxford, and of course Ryan Taylor, our centre forward from last season, had also joined Oxford in the close season. I'd not realised that Kitson had since retired, so had visions of our centre halves lining up against a double dollop of ginger. As it happened our defenders didn't require specially adapted sunglasses as Ryan Taylor had been benched after no goals in his first eight starts and Kitson was by now living off his Pompey administration payout.

The game itself was for long periods a fairly even affair,

with us having much of the possession but actually creating next to nothing in terms of chances, and Oxford having less possession but looking more threatening. They had signed a few decent quality players at this level and one of them, Liam Sercombe, signed from Exeter, struck in a half-volley to give them the lead in the latter stages of the first half. It could have been worse had Paul Jones not won a one on one just before half time to keep the margin down.

The second half followed a similar pattern to the first. We played some pretty stuff with little cutting edge until Adam McGurk picked up a pass, took a touch and smacked one in from 30 yards. Their keeper had been so taken by surprise at a shot, not least one on target, that he'd been slow to react and was well beaten. I suspect in fact that he'd been leaning against the other post smoking a fag and talking to his bird as if in Oxford Sunday League Div 4. Suffice to say that he was able to do this for the rest of the game as the only chances were at the other end. The game finished 1-1 and I felt it was a point gained rather than two lost. Oxford struck me as a decent side. Michael Appleton had always tried to send out a team to play football properly and he seemed to be reproducing this at Oxford. I felt that they would be near the top come the end of the season.

We exited the ground onto the rear concourse and turned right to get back to our car which was at the rear of the home stand. There seemed to be a large police presence and they were stopping anyone from passing that way, rather heavy-handedly I thought. We walked up to one police officer and said that we were going that way to our car. His reply was that we couldn't go through that way but had to walk all of the way around the other three sides of the stadium. Other people had obviously got the same message and some were getting shall we say a little fractious about being told that they had to walk all around the stadium rather than the 30 or 40 yards by the direct route. Looking around the car park at the stationary cars waiting to join the queue to exit meant that we weren't going anywhere fast, however, so we just turned round and strolled round the outside of the ground. I still couldn't see nonetheless what was the problem.

Policing at football grounds seems to vary from place to place. Some forces seem to have a knack of being able to control a crowd in a light-handed way but others seem to go out of their way to be hostile. I think it has something to do with the pre-conceptions amongst some forces that all visiting football supporters are thugs with no interest in just having a good day out. So hello Oxford Constabulary, we're not in the 1980s any more.

Some of the best crowd control techniques I have seen are at Wembley. Leaving the stadium to make your way up Wembley Way to the tube station means joining thousands of people jumping on a succession of trains back into central London. The police filter the movement to the trains by using mounted police. As the trains come in then the horses turn to face you, enabling you to pass between them, and when the station is full, the horses turn sideways to block the way until the next train comes through and the congestion eases. It's a simple technique which is made all the better because the senior mounted officer has a loud hailer and gives a constant, often humorous, briefing to those who are waiting, a bit like a Rugby Union referee constantly issuing a pre-emptive warning to a player to get away from a ruck.

I particularly remember our first FA Cup semi-final in 2008 when we beat West Brom. One of the Baggies fans was getting a bit strung up about the wait to get through to the station as the horses closed ranks once again. The voice came over the loud-hailer "enjoy the moment, you're not coming back" which prompted a few laughs and diffused the tension straight away.

Anyway, after the round the stadium Oxford half-marathon, we eventually got back to the car and joined the queue to get back on to the main road. By the time we finally got onto a piece of tarmac that a satnav would recognise, it must have been a good 45 minutes after we'd left the ground. Fortunately the road home was clear and I walked through the door in plenty of time to letch at the dancers (female ones anyway) on Strictly.

So would I want to be an Oxford fan? Would I want this to be my everyday match experience? Short answer no. There is something to be said for leaving your house an hour before a game, parking up and walking to the ground, maybe having a quick pint and a pie on the way. Would I want to have to get to the ground at 1 pm just to get a parking space, have little in the way of options for food and drink and have to wait at least 30 minutes before I could even get in the stadium? With fairly unfriendly police and stewards, to boot, no thank you, wouldn't be for me. Kirsty Allsop could try as hard as she liked but she wouldn't find any plusses here to sell to me. I hoped that Bristol the following Saturday would be an all round more satisfying experience.

CHAPTER 9

BRISTOL ROVERS

The group which went to Bristol Rovers was much the same as went to Cambridge earlier in the year. The exceptions were Steve and Sue who were going to further decimate Steve's retirement lump sum by having a weekend in Iceland. I suppose you could say that they'd be meeting a different type of geyser than us.

This was the Saturday of the England/Wales world cup rugby which was being played on the Saturday night, so we thought that Bristol would be an ideal place to have an overnighter. We booked into what we thought was the same Holiday Inn, but in fact it transpired that Andy and I had booked into a different Holiday Inn to Chop. This posed irreconcilable problems during the day ahead.

Chop was going up separately, so the decision between us was whether I or Andy would drive. It was a no-brainer really. Andy has spent his life having freebies on trains and apart from driving occasionally to Golf Days because he can't lug all that gear on a train, he rarely drives. In fact although he and Bev both work, they only have the one car which Bev uses to travel a couple of miles south on Portsea Island to get to work each day.

The other reason I was to drive is that Andy is not the most confident driver I know. It took him 4 attempts to pass his driving test. He had the same examiner each time. Apparently, on the fourth occasion the examiner sighed and told him "OK I'll pass you this time, but you need to get some practice". Once when a bunch of us were on a golf holiday, it was Andy's turn to drive us to the course. It must be the only time that I had ever seen someone have to do a 3-point turn on a roundabout. OK it was a small roundabout and we were in a minibus in Biarritz so not familiar surroundings but even so. I was accordingly quick to volunteer to drive on this occasion in the interests of Health and Safety.

We picked them up at about 9.15, Sarah the Satnav telling me that it was going to take just over two hours to get to our hotel on the outskirts of Bristol. It was a beautiful September day and the road was clear as we made our way up the A34 to Newbury and then along the M4. Just after Swindon the dreaded motorway gantry flashed up "50 animals in road". I slowed down, and Bev said "well, how do they know there are 50?" to which we had a little chuckle.

About a mile further on an HGV was parked up in the hard shoulder and the driver was ushering a couple of geese over the safety barrier by the side of the road. Bev said "well there are a couple of geese but I don't know how they get 50". We chuckled again.

About 10 minutes later and just 26 minutes from our hotel, Andy asked if we were having a pit-stop. I replied that we were only 26 minutes away, but he felt that he needed to err on the side of caution and we ended up stopping at the next service station around 10 miles down the road, where Andy relieved his creaking bladder and we grabbed a quick brunch. I had one of those sausage bean and cheese pasties from Greggs – I always think a strange concoction but I'm sold on them.

Whilst drinking our coffee by the car, we talked about the rather ostentatious and exaggerated animals in the road gantry warning. It was at this stage that Bev admitted that she really had thought that the sign meant that they had counted 50 animals in the road and not that 50 was the temporary speed limit. We cracked up laughing, this was a highly intelligent and efficient teacher at a local primary school, albeit blonde! However when we spoke about it more, it didn't seem so daft. She was married to a bloke with subsidised train travel so they would invariably travel any distance by train. Her own driving experience would be braving a couple of miles of queueing traffic north to south in Portsmouth, and she would rarely if ever see a motorway, nor understand the significance of gantry messages which the rest of us saw every day with some monotony.

Sixteen minutes later – exactly as Sarah had predicted – we arrived at our hotel. It was too early to check-in but Andy felt the need to use the hotel facilities again as a precaution before we started our trek towards the ground. I'd checked the map and it didn't look too far from our hotel. We walked past Chop's Holiday Inn by Express and stopped to text him to join us if he and Toni had arrived as well. Waiting 5 minutes with no response and turning left following signs for the Memorial Stadium, we embarked on what we hoped would be a short walk to the ground preceded by a pleasant hour in a nearby hostelry garden. It turned out that I had seriously underestimated the distance, to the extent that I reckon I should have sought sponsorship for my favoured charity for the length of the walk.

Hostelries seemed in short supply, but we passed numerous churches of virtually every denomination. I wondered if the good people of Bristol were all teetotal, and I half expected a few Amish carriages to drive by. Alternatively it may well be that there was still a feeling of guilt about Bristol being the centre of the British slave trade, and like the British Government apologising all over the world for the evil deeds of Disraeli and Palmerston (in another 100 years it will probably be Blair), they were still seeking atonement.

We finally reached an area which was more commercial than residential, passed a couple of pubs that had signs saying "no colours" which ruled out me and Andy, before we came upon the Queen Vic, a large pub on the main road which I remembered reading was not too far from the ground. We made for the bar like we'd just crossed the Sahara. On the way to the bar we passed another school mate Tim, primarily an Everton fan but a regular at Fratton Park when a free ticket was on offer. He was in Bristol because his wife Jo was visiting one of those wedding exhibitions with her future daughter in law and Tim was with his lad and some other friends going to the game.

The beauty of the World Cup in any sport is that breweries bring out new beers (or more likely re-brand old ones) but whatever, I ordered a pint of Try Line or Scrum Down or something like that, which proved to be rather moreish, a bit like White Chocolate Dairy Crunch, a bar of which I can see off without blinking. We'd decamped to the very pleasant and sun-drenched pub garden, where we embarked on a game of telephone voicemail tag with Chop and Toni who by now had arrived in Bristol and were looking to hook up. At the same time I was exchanging texts and voicemails with Keith, an ex-business partner and regular golf acquaintance who was also in Bristol for the game with his three boys, the eldest of whom had just started at University there.

Now this is why middle-aged men should not be let loose on mobile telephones. By 2 o'clock I had 9 voicemail messages and had probably left the same number in return. I had a new 'phone and hadn't yet worked out how to work the volume and vibrate functions properly. As a result the messages were getting more and more irate – "Where are you? Switch on your bloody 'phone you moron!"

Keith texted to say that he was in the Queen Vic. Having scoured the pub I texted him back to say that he wasn't. About

20 minutes later he entered the pub garden with a sheepish look and explained that his son had taken him to another Queen Vic, or something of a similar name, which was down on the Quays about 5 miles away.

Keith was gloating though because he had managed to get seats whereas we had only managed to get terrace tickets. He couldn't understand why we hadn't got seats before they sold out, because he'd seen Steve just ahead of him in the queue when the tickets went on sale. Steve had told me that the bloke in front of him in the queue had bagged the last seats So in turn I suggested to Keith that he'd best check his own tickets. He pulled the envelope from his jacket pocket and his face dropped when he realised he was on the terrace as well.

At this point I returned the gloating. Keith is about 5 foot 4 and I asked him whether he'd brought along his milk crate to stand on. It got us talking about when we got taken to Fratton Park when we were kids and your parents took milk crates to the ground for you to stand on to see the game. I remembered specifically a 3rd round FA Cup game against the Arsenal double winning side of 1971 when I was standing on a crate behind the Milton End goal when Mike Trebilcock lashed in a last minute equaliser. My Mum and Dad got in trouble with my school for taking me out of school for the afternoon on the day of the replay.

Keith eventually tired of being mocked for being vertically challenged, and disappeared with his boys in tow like something out of the Von Trapp family. We eventually gave up on any sort of rendezvous with Chop and Toni after yet further vitriolic voicemail exchanges, and made our way to the Memorial Ground which was about 10 minute walk away.

This was my first visit to Bristol Rovers latest ground. I'd been to a game at the old Eastville Stadium in the early 80s and it had been a painful experience. Standing on an open terrace in the pissing rain, we'd got thumped 5-1. I hoped today's experience would be better. At least it was tee-shirt weather.

The Memorial Stadium is a bit of a curate's egg. The away terrace is situated in what I think is the south-east corner of the ground and takes up about a third of one side. It is located next to a home stand which runs much of the rest of the way along that side. The opposite side of the ground was taken up by a home stand with seating above terracing and what looked like hospitality boxes at the top. The home stand was at the end to our right, and the limited number of away seats were at the end to our left. It looked like it had been put up as a temporary effort, had the look of an Andersen shelter, and would not have looked out of place at a Wessex League ground. It only took up about the centre of the end so about half of one end of the stadium was completely undeveloped. All told it was a stadium that a 5 year old might have put together with Duplo bricks but had me feeling somewhat disorientated.

We queued up at a fairly efficiently run food stand which dispensed meal deals for about 6 quid, but that included a humungous and tasty pasty, bag of crisps, bar of chocolate and a soft drink, so we weren't left feeling ripped off.

It seemed strange to be standing on a terrace again to watch a match. It must have been 15-20 years since my last terrace experience, though there had in between been many games both home and away where I'd been obliged to stand in a seated area to see the action. We hadn't got to the ground early enough to secure a place leaning on a stanchion and I suspected my ageing knees and vulnerable lower back would be feeling the strain by half-time.

We heard the team news and noted that Conor Chaplin, our teenage mutant hero local youth team product, who'd already scored goals in two League Cup ties against higher opposition, was going to start the game behind Jayden Stockley. Our playmaker Gary Roberts was on the bench.

Bristol Rovers had gone out of the league for a season but had got their League status back within a year. I was pleased about that. They had played us a couple of seasons back in one of their last games before relegation, and had sold out the Milton end at Fratton Park which was unusual in this division. Although they had lost 3-2 that day and were relegated soon afterwards, the whole club just seemed to me to have a bit more character than their City neighbours. Even their nickname the "Gas" (apparently due to the gasworks next to the old Eastville Stadium) preserved a sort of individuality.

Inside the ground, we finally ended the telephone tag with Chop and joined him, Toni and their daughter Mel on the terrace.

We started the game more crisply than we had against Oxford though it soon became clear that Bristol were not as good a side as the Oxford we'd played the previous week. Whereas our football was neat and along the ground, Bristol used the long ball much more, hoping to hit much-travelled striker Jermaine Easter but he was getting little change out of our defence.

After a couple of slick moves when we had come close, we finally broke the deadlock when Gareth Evans nodded home a right wing cross, and it stayed that way until half-time. We sat down on the terracing and had a chat, feeling pretty confident of an away win as we hadn't seen much to trouble our goal. That complacency ended within a couple of minutes of the re-start when Easter got first to a near post right wing cross and his flick hit the crossbar and the ball trickled over the line off the back of our prostrate keeper. It was at this point that I noticed the small electronic scoreboard on the opposite stand. It was like a Twitter scoreboard because it clearly only had room for a small number of letters. It just tweeted "Gas 1 Pom 1"

The tide had turned temporarily and a long shot then hit the outside of our post. Cook had seen enough. On came Roberts in place of Conor Chaplin, who in this game had buzzed around without achieving an end product, and the game turned our way again. Roberts started to control possession despite the close attentions of Rovers' terrier like midfielder with the pony-tail, whose name I never quite caught. With about 15 minutes left a flowing move ended with a great cross which tempted the keeper, but Stockley got there first and jabbed the ball past him for what was to prove the winner.

We left the ground content in the knowledge that we were at the top of the promotion places, and with two home games to follow, with every chance of opening up a gap at the top of the table.

I'd quite enjoyed my day on the terraces and as we walked away from the ground it occurred to me that standing has its' advantages and I now turn to one of my biggest bugbears; people who leave football matches before the final whistle. If you're standing and someone decides to leave early it makes little difference, you just carry on watching the match undisturbed. But it affects me a great deal at our home matches where I sit at the end of a row in the Fratton End. I can quite accept having to be up and down in my seat for those who are seated later than me, particularly for evening games, perhaps because they've rushed from work. I can also accept the same people getting to a food stand queue early before half-time because they haven't had chance to eat for the same reason. On a night match I realise that transport issues mean that people may have to catch the last train to an obscure village near Bognor Regis or the last ferry to the Isle of Wight. What I don't understand is people paying to watch 90 minutes football at 3p.m on a Saturday and then leaving as much as 10 to 15 minutes before the end, disturbing my enjoyment in the process.

Let's put it another way. Would I dream of leaving a showing of Les Miserables in a London theatre 15 minutes early (even though like most people I know the ending). Of course not.

What about TV? Can you really think of going into work the day after the last in series Game of Thrones episode saying that you'd decided to go to bed 5 minutes before the end because you had to get up for work the next day?

Likewise, imagine this conversation:-

"I went to the pictures last night to see The Sixth Sense"

"Did you enjoy it?"

"It was alright but I didn't really see the point of it. Mind, I left ten minutes before the end because I wanted to avoid the crowds leaving Gunwharf.".

Football is much like The Sixth Sense – you really don't know what twists there are going to be in the last few minutes. Just think if you were a Man United fan who'd left the 1999 Champions League final 5 minutes before the end or one of those Liverpool fans who left the stadium in Istanbul at half-time in 2005. Don't do it and don't disturb me in the process, unless you're one of those people who can't help but boo at even the most entertaining 0-0 draw, in which case you have my permission, indeed encouragement, to bugger off early.

We strolled back to the Vic and sampled another pint of Penalty Try, having a friendly dismemberment of the match with some Gasheads before deciding how we were getting back to the hotel. I crossed the road to a bus stop but established that none of the buses on this route were going close to our hotel, so Bev tried using her Uber app which she'd downloaded on to her 'phone a few weeks earlier but not yet tried. She entered our location and got a text back saying that Mohammed would be with us in 3 minutes and 46 seconds in a taupe coloured Toyota. It even gave us Mohammed's mug shot. Whilst a few seconds out, they were true to their word and he traced the route back to our hotel by the same route we'd walked, making us realise how far that had been.

While at the game we had discussed where we would meet up to watch the rugby that night. Chop had got a recommendation for a pub called the White Horse in Clifton. We had no idea where it was or how far away but arranged to meet them there, with Belinda and Brad, who were also out on the town, at 7.30.

Our Holiday Inn was pleasant enough, though at £109 a night it came in a bit steeper than the average Premier Inn with no better facilities really. As I took my shower I looked at the usual notice asking you to place the towels back on the rail and use them again in the interests of the Company's Environmental Corporate Social Responsibility. In my mind I translate this notice to "We are trying to cut down on our annual laundry bill. Please help us to do this by using your towels again and again".

I wondered if the Holiday Inn Chief Executive adopts this policy as he walks home to Hampstead Heath each evening. "Darling, from now onwards I feel that I must take the lead in bringing the Company's environmental policy into our personal household so I shall be wearing the same pair of brogs three days running and cutting down on the detergent entering our eco-system".

"But what about the skidmarks dear? You know how you suffer terribly. What if you have an accident or get rushed to hospital? I should be so embarrassed. And we're going to the MacKenzie-Smith's for canapes tomorrow night."

"No matter. It's all dictated by our environmental policy which must prevail at all times. Two pairs of cacks a week it is"

Yeah, you bet.

We met Bev and Andy in reception and experimented with Uber again. Sure enough, 5 minutes later our carriage arrived, but it took about 25 minutes to get us across what looked like a thriving city centre and over to Clifton. My lips went dry at the thought of how much this taxi ride was costing so I was pleasantly surprised to reach our destination for £16.

The pub was large, modern and packed to the rafters. Being close to the border it contained a mix of English and Welsh rugby fans which made for a buzzing atmosphere, and there were big screens throughout the whole pub. The only free tables were reserved for those who were going to have food and although none of us was unduly hungry after our Memorial Stadium Megafeast, the women wanted to grab a seat so we ordered something with chips and watched the match at an acute angle, a bit like the penalties which Dan Biggar seemed to be knocking over for the Welsh in a very tight game.

Songs alternated from Swing Low to Bread of Heaven in the pub as the game swung one way and then the other. Still no sign of Chop until a text told us that they'd got back to their hotel late after the match, had not reached the White Horse until 8.30 and were turned away because it was full. They were in another pub down the street.

It was near the end of the game and we were staying put. Then came that crucial and awful moment when England were awarded a penalty in the last few minutes. Trailing by 3 points, would Chris Robshaw opt for what seemed like an easy 3 points and take the draw or go for the try and a win?

He went bravely, perhaps stupidly, for the latter, but would he really know that his lineout would dissolve like Pygmies and his hooker throw the ball like a ten year old girl on Sports Day? Cheers turned to groans and the white shirts left the pub en masse like it was a Sunderland home game.

Having at last a bit of space to move around I went outside onto perhaps the biggest area of outside seating I'd ever seen. And it was no wonder they made the most of it. The decking overlooked the Avon Gorge and the view up to the floodlit

Clifton Bridge was impressive. I finished my pint in peaceful reflection of the surroundings and we made our way down the road to join the others.

The Portcullis in Clifton Village is a quirky but fantastic pub. Just like pubs used to be. There were two entrances, one on a sort of ground-cum-basement floor and another by going up a few steps to the top floor. We went up the stairs and found Chop and the others around a large table. They'd watched the rugby on a portable screen. It was a bit like one of those screens which your parents put up to show their holiday slides through a projector. Board games from virtually ceiling to floor were stacked in the corner and Chop couldn't wait to tell us about the awesome beer on offer. I went down some rickety steps to the bar area where there was a row of real ale taps mostly from Dawkins brewery. One of them was 9.8% proof and could only be bought in half-pints at a time. Chop dared me but I remembered a beer festival from a few years back where my last ticket had been spent upon a half of aptly named Skullsplitter at similar alcohol content. Conscious that I would be driving home the following morning I resisted the pressure, opting for something a little less powerful.

There were about half a dozen customers in the downstairs bar. They were either chatting to the landlady, reading newspapers or doing Sudoku. No jukeboxes or fruit machines. We spent the last hour of the evening chatting about the football and the rugby, supping some great beer.

Chop explained that they had not got back to their hotel until about 7.30, having hopped on a bus which had taken them on a tour of Bristol and then close to the Welsh border before it had got remotely close to their hotel. They hadn't eaten and at closing time, as we exited on to the streets of Clifton, they walked off towards the town in the hope of finding a curry house, whilst we opted to get back to the hotel.

Bev was put in charge of finding us a taxi and she checked

in on good old Uber again. She told us that the message back was that demand was currently high and that taxi prices were currently running at two and a half times daytime cost. Remembering we'd paid £16 to get there we weren't keen to pay £40 to get back so Bev and Andy tried a few local firms. Michelle and I looked in the local estate agents window and realised that we would not be able to afford to downsize to a flat in Clifton – not surprisingly because it has some majestic town houses.

I also pondered on how careers can founder on luck. No doubt Chris Robshaw would be absolutely pilloried in the morning papers for his decision to go for the win rather than the draw. Yet the same papers would have been lauding him as inspirational had the lineout resulted in a try. Some people are, I think, just lucky

Pete – see Cheltenham chapter – is one of those people whose golf drives invariably rattle around in trees only to emerge into the middle of the fairway. He once hit a stray tee-shot on a par 3 in our Club Championship which hit another mate Rob on his shaved pate while he was standing on the next tee. Rob was disorientated and bleeding for the rest of the day, whilst Pete, whose ball had bounced off Rob's head on to the green, knocked in the birdie putt.

And what about history? I wonder what we would now be saying about Wellington's decision to match up with Napoleon at Waterloo had his mate Marshall Blucher decided to stop off for a Lowenbrau and Bratwurst lunch rather than riding at full speed to meet his old buddy and snatch victory from the jaws of defeat.

It struck me that the old myth that luck evens itself out was very much a myth. The one exception I could think of is Sean Bean. Barely making half way in virtually any film or TV series, his luck evens up in Sharpe when he's run through about 15 times but always emerges like a bionic man to beat shit out of the Frogs.

These thoughts were interrupted by Bev saying that the earliest taxi we could get elsewhere would be 1.30. We went back to Uber who said that Gustav would be with us in 5 minutes, although we realised it would be at great expense. I supposed that it was a bit like a 24 hour plumber who advertises a horrendous call out fee to come out at an unsocial hour to fix your boiler in a cold snap. The difference being that when you ring the plumber it invariably goes to voicemail whereas at least Gustav turned up on time, even if he did relieve us of £38 in the process.

We'd had a great day in Bristol, admittedly largely based around sport and beer. The only part of the Town Centre I'd seen had been the parts we'd flashed past in our taxi ride but it certainly looked like a stylish place where I'd be happy to pay a return visit.

Finishing off with a coffee from the in-house Costa at the hotel, we left early for home the next day, thankfully encountering not even one, let alone 50, animals on the M4.

CHAPTER 10

CARLISLE

There's something to be said for being a MK Dons fan. Not much, in fact I can't think of anything. History, tradition maybe? No, of course I jest.

The only advantage that I can see is that whilst a Dons fan is looking at a maximum 4 hour journey pretty much anywhere, if you are a Plymouth or Carlisle supporter then you have some pretty lengthy trips to places completely at the other end of the country. But then again I doubt that MK Dons have much away support. Why would you want to look at real cows on your travels when you have the plastic variety to look at every day?

You have to admire a fan who will travel 6 or 7 hours for a Tuesday night game in the middle of January. I can recall a game last season when we played Accrington Stanley, who were at the time in the mid to lower regions of League Two, and a couple of coachloads of supporters made the trip to Fratton on a wet and windy night, to be treated to a dreary 0-0 draw.

My least favourite football chant is "Your support is f…… shit". The usual suspects trotted it out on this particular night and it just seemed disrespectful and embarrassing. You need to be pretty hardy to be a supporter of a club which spends its' life in the lower divisions and you'd expect that a level of mutual respect might exist. At least we've had seasons in the higher leagues, but if you are a lifelong Hartlepool fan you haven't had much cause for celebration over the years and to keep making long trips to Plymouth is impressive dedication.

Coming back from our last Premier League game at Everton, we stopped off for a break at Warwick services. There were coachloads of Manchester United shirts as the Man U southern supporters trooped back to Guildford (I suppose unlike Howard the armchair fan they can say they've at least been to Old Trafford, mind). Anyway, next most prolific were the Pompey shirts but there were also a couple of coachloads of supporters in neon yellow shirts with a logo which I didn't recognise. I got chatting to a couple and they were from a Conference team, I think it was Telford United, and they'd been playing somewhere like Dartford or Ebbsfleet.. I had assumed that as there were so many of them it was a big game, but no, they weren't getting in the play-offs or anything like that, it was just a run of the mill end of season game. I wondered how many of the United fans would be travelling to places like Ebbsfleet if they dropped to the Conference. Not many I suspect.

I thought about this as I 'phoned to get my Carlisle tickets. It would be a 7 to 8 hour journey from Portsmouth and probably the only people who would make this trip were the diehards, the stupid, Northern Pompey ex-pats or those like me who decided to combine it with a couple of days in the Lake District with the missus. Some people might find it strange going to football with the wife, especially one who doesn't really care much for football, but from her perspective she gets a weekend away from the household drudge of washing and ironing. From mine, I get the benefit of being accompanied to football by someone who has not seen us lose home or away for two and a half seasons. And in view of the many defeats we'd sustained over that period, it made her a lucky charm for me.

I booked a really good value two nights bed and breakfast for under £120 at the Ennerdale Hall hotel just outside the national park, and thought it would be nice if we could hook up with Michelle's sister Denise and brother-in-law Michael for the weekend. On the basis that they live in Durham we only see them two or three times a year and I figured it wouldn't be too arduous a trek for them. Sure enough I soon had a text back saying that they had booked the same break, and it was later decided that the women would have a long lunch on the Saturday, whilst Michael would come to football with me.

We've always got on well and the previous season we'd happened to visit them on probably the worst football weekend possible. Mike is a Mackem and on the weekend of our visit it was the weekend when Sunderland were playing at Southampton. We were away at Bury. Settling down to watch Soccer Saturday, we watched the video printer start to go berserk and there were visits seemingly every 5 minutes to St. Marys as Sunderland gradually slipped to an 8-0 defeat. Pompey lost 3-0 so with a combined aggregate defeat of 11-0 we consigned ourselves to beer for the rest of the day.

Our next visit to Durham was towards the end of the season, when Sunderland were due to play the Stains at home in the reverse fixture and Mike got a couple of tickets in the hope that a watching Pompey fan would have a detrimental effect upon our south coast rivals. I'm pleased to say that I threw myself in to being a Mackem for the day, and Sunderland won 2-1 though to be honest I don't know how because they were pretty much second best for most of the game.

A week or so before the Carlisle game I Googled Carlisle United to find out a bit more about the ground and their players. About half way down the second page on Google I saw the name Davie Irons, and read an article which referred to him as their Assistant Manager in 2013. I looked on his Wikipedia page and realised that he was the same guy I'd played with while at Newcastle in 1980. I knew he'd played a few games for Queen of the South when he was a youngster but then when he'd come to Polytechnic he had spent a few years out of Scottish football, instead playing for the Poly on a Saturday in the North-East Amateur League, which wasn't a bad standard up there. We put together a good run in this particular season, and Dave Irons had been a treat to play with. He had a cultured left foot and worked the left side of the pitch with great skill, mesmerising most defenders at this level.

Come the end of the season, we were in the frame to win the League having won 19 out of 23 games. There was one left which was to be against Hylton CW who had a similar record. Back in those days there were a lot of Colliery Welfare (CW) teams playing at a pretty high level. Basically they were teams affiliated to the social clubs of the various sizeable pits which were still going strong up in the North-East before Maggie came along and decimated whole communities in the 1980s. It wasn't unknown for these teams to get into the First round proper of the FA Cup, I seem to remember Easington CW did so more than once.

Hylton was about the roughest part of Sunderland and we realised when we played them at home that these boys were not to be messed with. They had little finesse and if there was one game when it would be suicidal to wear gloves or white boots, this was it. As well as having Norman Hunter and Ron Harris tendencies, they also had some pretty tasty players as well, so we knew it wasn't going to be a cakewalk. We'd also been told by other teams in the league that Hylton's ground was a pretty intimidating place to spend a Saturday afternoon.

Our team was picked accordingly. One of our most skilful players was a lad called Steve Warriner who'd played in Boro's youth team, but Warriner was unlikely to be cut out for this game, being one of those guys who wore his shorts high up on his waist and then squinnied when the opposition selected him for special treatment. Dave Irons was going to be left midfield on the basis that he just got up after a heavy challenge and got on with it. Often in fact the opposition didn't get close enough to make a heavy challenge, he was that good at this level.

We arrived at the ground and it was, surprisingly in view of the fact that it was a league decider, sparsely populated with the spectators being about a dozen old boys and a whippet. We had expected hostility on and off the pitch so were pleasantly surprised that the only hazard was bollock-high tackles. Having conceded an early goal we recovered and went in 2- 1 up at half – time, commenting in the changing room that we didn't know what all the fuss was about with the opposing supporters.

Emerging for the second half, the penny dropped. It was about 3.15, the bar had closed at the social club and 200 pissed-up miners were now around the pitch. The fact that we were students meant that we got treatment probably worse than most other teams. We weren't exactly queueing up to take the throw-ins. Somehow notwithstanding the intimidation, we kept the score at 2-1 until about 10 minutes from the end when Dave Irons weaved down the left and put over a cross that was right on my noddle in the centre of the goal 6 yards out. I went up for it knowing I was going to score when I got a shove in the back of such force that I ended in the back of the net myself. It was the most stonewall pen you'll ever see yet I didn't think the ref would risk giving it, but to my amazement he did and Davie Irons despatched the kick.

We saw out the last 10 minutes and Steve Warriner came on for Davie. He'd been squinnying on the sidelines at every tackle and when he took Davie's place on the left-wing I remember one of their players running from the far side of the pitch to stick his finger up Warriner's nose and saying "I'm gonna have you, yer fuckin'poof". The next 10 minutes were hilarious. I don't think Steve touched the ball. He was too busy impersonating Colin Jackson in the 110 metre hurdles as challenges came in chest-high.

As the whistle blew we legged it to the changing rooms where we gathered up our gear and jumped into the minibus (which had backed up to the changing room doors) with our football kit still on. The driver revved up the engine and we escaped the gauntlet of miners in crombies who'd each drunk a gallon of Vaux Special at lunch time. I never saw the ref again. I don't know whether he survived but I bet he didn't hang around for his match fee. It was truly my scariest local football experience.

Wikipedia told me that Davie had gone on to play for several Scottish clubs including Partick, and had managed others including Morton. He was currently manager at Stranraer. In contrast after returning to Pompey I reached the heady heights of Dockyard Premier League. Mind, the gulf in talent was there for all to see.

I was also reminded, along similar lines, of a story told by one of my Dockyard League team- mates Andy Vernon. Andy had become an area sales manager for Walkers crisps and he told the story of when he'd met Gary Lineker at one of their London conferences. He said the conversation went something like this:- Andy: "Played against you once. Pompey boys v Leicester boys 1976." Gary: "Really? That's funny. I don't remember you. But amazing how we ended up working for the same Company".

I'd not been to the last three away games. I avoided Cambridge having taken the view that I couldn't surpass the previous year's scoreline, but we did half as well by winning 3-1, followed by Newport. I've never found Welsh football fans unduly friendly, and remembering Newport as a bit of a dump gave it a miss. I'd been there once before on the way back from a holiday in Wales and remember us winning 3-0. If I remember rightly, Kevin Dillon scored on his debut – he went on to become our most successful ever penalty taker. Maybe if someone had suggested we combine it with a weekend at Celtic Manor I might have been tempted. It sounded a pretty dire game but we won 1-0. The last game in October was Notts County. I would have liked to have gone to the oldest club in the League but before the fixture list had come out we had booked and paid to go to a charity Hallowe'en Ball north of Winchester. As it happened Notts County became our first away defeat of the season as we went down 2-1.

By the time Carlisle came around we'd slipped out of the automatic promotion spots. The problem was our home form, where we'd lost to Exeter the Tuesday after Bristol Rovers and had then drawn at home, without scoring, against Yeovil, Mansfield and Wimbledon. A last minute Stevenage equaliser meant another 1-1 draw, and our failure to win in front of our own crowd was becoming a major obstacle. I felt that we were missing two key players in our keeper Paul Jones and playmaker Gary Roberts, the latter I suspect having been the kingpin around which Paul Cook had planned the season. Both were now out with medium term injuries. A lot of fans also felt that Danny Hollands' re-emergence to partner the ever-reliable Michael Doyle in our defensive midfield was a negative move, but Nigel Atangana, who was a more attacking influence, seemed out of favour.

Cook was obviously unhappy about his striking options once Jayden Stockley was also injured and he clearly didn't feel that Matt Tubbs fitted his preferred system which really called for a stronger hold-up player as lone striker. He dipped into the loan market for Caolan Lavery from Sheffield Wednesday, then nipped across the other half of Sheffield for Mark McNulty, who had a decent scoring record at a higher level.

In early November I had a flush out and cartilage repair on my football knee. It was two weeks before our Carlisle trip and we decided that it was best if Michelle did the bulk of the driving. Aiming to get to our Lake District hotel about 5 on the Friday, we left about 10 and made good time to our first coffee break at Warwick services. On the basis that I wanted to be using the clutch as little as possible, I volunteered to drive the next stretch which was all motorway. It took little time to get to the northern end of the M6 toll road but the satnav was highlighting an accident and tailbacks on the M6 around junction 17. Ten minutes later the gantry told us that the M6 was now closed between 16 and 17 so we trusted Sarah to take us on a detour. It was to be 6 hours before we finally got to Preston, and I'd driven 84 miles in 5 hours. My foot had been up and down on the clutch in stop start traffic like a yoyo. By the time we stopped for a comfort break Michelle virtually had to carry me into the service station.

I'd vowed about 6 months before that I'd never again travel north on a Friday, after it had taken us 10 hours to get to Newcastle. The M6 is even worse than the M1 and by the time we had got back on the motorway after the closure, we'd hit the Lancashire conurbation at rush hour, moving at a snail's pace until we got past Wigan. I reminded myself that with Morecambe and Accrington coming up in January, I should put a big sign up in the house NEVER to drive north again on a Friday.

We'd booked in for dinner at the hotel for 8. Michael and Denise had already arrived but bearing in mind it was 7.15 when we stopped at Preston we were never going to get across to the west coast before the kitchen closed at 9, so we texted them to crack on. But when we eventually got to the hotel just after 9 we were grateful to find that they had kept the kitchen open. We dumped our bags in reception and stuck a pin in the menu just pleased not to be ending our day with a cheese sandwich. After a meal that was not completely relaxing after the stressful travelling, we discussed the following day's plan of action. One option was for us to take one car to Carlisle and leave the other one with the women. The other was to jump on a train from Whitehaven to Carlisle. We plumped for the latter.

So after a full English the following morning, we had an hour to spare before our train and decided to drive the short distance to St. Bees which is the start of the coast to coast walk from the Lake District to Scarborough. We'd already noticed that the temperature had dropped 10 degrees over the last 24 hours, and the car park at St. Bees was near deserted when we arrived. Being a responsible citizen I none the less paid the £1.10 to park for an hour. We walked down to the promenade; the tide was out and I looked out on a quite superb stretch of sand which was however populated only by dog walkers. The views over the Solway Firth to Scotland were spectacular but with the wind whipping down from the north our stay was short and legging it back to the car quickly I calculated we'd paid 22p a minute to park.

It was a short drive to Whitehaven and the wives dropped us off at the station in plenty of time to catch the 11.38 to Carlisle. There were a mixed group waiting on the platform. Some were obviously going to do a bit of Christmas shopping, but there were a fair smattering of all-male groups. A lone Pompey shirt belonged to a lad in his mid-20s. It got me wondering where these guys come from. Was he a Northern Pompey fan, or perhaps alternatively visiting friends? For a League Two side we certainly seem to have fans in far-flung corners.

The train was just two carriages and it had started its journey at Barrow, having taken an hour already to crawl up the coast to Whitehaven. It was pretty full, but we found a couple of those seats which have notices asking you to give them up to older people. Looking around the carriage we were as close to qualifying as anyone so rather than leave them empty, we parked ourselves down in a position whereby we could look down the carriage.

The journey of 30 miles was to take about an hour and ten minutes, and as we left Whitehaven I realised why. The train ran next to the shoreline for about the first ten miles. It was really very picturesque, but I could understand, remembering the collapse of a similar railway line in Devon the year before, why the train crawled along at about 20 miles an hour over this stretch. On the one side the beach, on the other views across the mountains which had received their first snowfall of the winter the night before. It would be hard to call it boring.

But after the train had gone past Workington, the landscape became more industrial, so I looked down the full carriage and the first thing that struck me was that we were about the only people who weren't drinking alcohol in some shape or form. The groups of men, presumably on the way to the football or rugby, were supping Budweisers and McEwans Special. The lone Pompey fan had struck up conversation with some Carlisle fans. But the most striking group was what we christened the Orange Hen Party. This was a group of girls in their late teens to early twenties who had all obviously seen a few hours on the sunbed in the preceding week because they all had the same complexion. They were going for it big- time with the Orange Lambrini presumably to match their skin pigment. One of them was applying make-up like a seasoned plasterer, using her mobile as a mirror The others must have got up in the middle of the night to apply their war paint.

We wondered what they would be like by closing time, but then overhearing a nearby conversation realised why they were out so early. The last two trains back from Carlisle leave at 8.15 and 9.45 pm, and apparently both are dry trains. So if you are going back down the coast, you've had your last drink on your day out by about half-nine at latest. I wondered if the night clubs opened at 4 o'clock in the afternoon to cater for this.

Carlisle station was impressive. It had a high glass roof reminiscent of the classic London Victorian stations and as a building it put its compatriots in the cities of Hampshire, for example, to shame. I guessed that it carried a lot of trains through to Glasgow which accounted for its' size compared to its population.

Carlisle might punch above its weight in the station stakes but the town itself is fairly ordinary in comparison. Not a dump by any means, but it had little to distinguish it from any other large town. We left the station, had a quick look at the shopping centre to our right which contained the usual chain-store suspects, and decided to sample the delights of the cask ales at The Griffin pub which was the closest to the station and about a mile away from the ground.

It was half empty when we ordered our first pint, but within 5 minutes it was packed out with probably the largest stag party I'd seen. Their accents were all Scottish and I assumed they had hopped over the border from Annan or somewhere closer to Carlisle than Glasgow. I was glad I was not in the queue behind the guy who had the kitty, else I might still have been thirsty by the time I left for the match.

Leaving about 2 o'clock to make our way to the ground, Mike opted for some fish and chips from the fish bar opposite which was staffed by the most oily and suave Italian you can imagine. Presumably he'd be shutting up shop mid-afternoon to prey on the Orange hen party. I decided to wait until I got to the ground, for food that is, not to prey on the hen party.

We walked along the main road past some impressive converted houses which were now occupied by estate agents, trendy looking wine bars and restaurants. The commercial district gradually thinned out to residential, and we passed Carlisle Rugby Club before arriving at Brunton Park next door. There was a statue outside the ground, but no, it wasn't George Best, Stanley Matthews or Billy Wright, just plain old Hughie McIlmoyle who obviously qualified as Carlisle's most famous player. Still, even then it was better than the first statue of Ted Bates at Southampton, where he looked more like a Munchkin from the Wizard of Oz than Ted Bates.

The first port of call for me was the nearest burger van. This had various meal deals varying in complexity and while in the queue with nothing else to do I mulled over my options. Arriving at the front I plumped for the pie meal deal but pies were apparently yesterday's news. So it came down to cheeseburger, cheeseburger or cheeseburger. In a moment of inspiration I opted for cheeseburger which was served by a youth so heavily pockmarked I became concerned as to my wellbeing. I worried that he may not have washed his hands having squeezed one of the many Vesuvius like tumuli that were sprouting from his face like the nearby Langdale Pikes. Sometimes a vivid imagination can destroy a cultured culinary experience and this was one of those occasions.

We took our seats in the away area, which ran half way along the length of the pitch, and the stand was uniform and comfortable enough. The word uniform was not vocabulary which could be applied to the other stands. The one opposite us in particular was a bit like the stand at Bristol. It looked like rather than demolishing one side and rebuilding, bits had just been added on as and when money became available, supposedly to make it look bigger and better. In that sense it was like the Katie Price of football stadiums.

I looked around my fellow fans and what struck me was the eclectic nature of the 954 souls who'd made the longest trip in our league season. There were plenty in their twenties but there were also lots of dads with kids, and a significant number you suspect could have named our 1949 and 1950 First Division championship team.

We started with our normal back six, Lavery up front and behind him Kyle Bennett, Adam McGurk and Gareth Evans. That makes 10 and a full team in a Chris Kamara commentary, but yes we also had a goalie. From the kick off it seemed clear that there was an appetite to get in Carlisle's faces high up the pitch which in my humble opinion had been one of the reasons why we had enjoyed early season success. In the first 10 minutes, a cross from the right found Lavery in acres of space 6 yards out but he couldn't direct his header other than straight at the Carlisle 'keeper. From the resulting corner we nearly scored again with a last ditch clearance preventing us taking the lead. For the rest of the half we dominated completely, but with insufficient cutting edge. It was inevitable that sooner or later Carlisle would put a move together and just before half time, a neat flick sent their left back scampering past our defence to be brought down by Christian Burgess on the edge of the box. It looked a foul all day long but very much borderline as to whether it was in the area. The referee (one Scott Duncan, or was it Duncan Scott – anyway he had a sort of Spoonerist name) had no hesitation in pointing to the spot and said left back stepped up to lash the ball past Murphy. Within minutes the half-time whistle blew and our players trudged off clearly unable to comprehend how they were walking off a goal down. There were 954 souls sloping off for a piddle and thinking the same thing.

At half-time we noticed the most striking and individual aspect of Brunton Park – their floodlights. They are mounted on a traditional stanchion but the lights rather than being at the top were lit half way up in a sort of triangular arrangement, shaped like a Christmas tree. In fact I said to Michael that with Christmas coming, there would be no need at Carlisle FC to put lights on the Christmas tree. All you'd need to do is shove the Christmas tree up the stanchion. Job done.

The second half opened much as the first had done and we

were pressing hard for an equaliser. Ben Davies made his way down the right and cut inside his defender in the corner of the penalty area, to be brought down a good yard or two inside the penalty area. The dashing Mr. Duncan was just 10 yards away with a clear view but inexplicably decided that it was a yard outside the box. How he could make a more borderline decision to give a penalty to the home side and then refuse to give a more clear cut penalty to the away side smacked of loss of bottle. Otherwise, I expect to see him in the next "Should have gone to Specsavers" advert. Even Michael as a neutral commented that the decision was perverse.

Back in the 70s we would have heard the chant "send the ref to Vietnam, Hallelujah" These days a ref would bite your arm off for a couple of weeks lazing on the beach at Na Trang. How times change. I did wonder how long it would be before someone rejuvenated this chant with a 2015 cover version substituting Syria for Vietnam. Or at Fulham, who must have the most knowledgeable and middle class fans in the country, maybe "send the ref to East Timor".

Nothing came of the free kick and on came Ben Tollitt and Mark McNulty. Within 10 minutes both made a difference, Tollitt beating his full-back to send in a low cross which Caolan Lavery bundled over the line, and within two minutes McNulty robbing their holding midfielder, striding forward and firing a shot into the corner. The game had turned around, and the substitutions were inspired but the next one was less so as McNulty was subbed after picking up a knock to be replaced by a third holding midfielder in Nigel Atangana, which handed Carlisle the initiative. Those who'd been at Carlisle the year before had seen this all before as we went 1-0 down, 2-1 up and then let in an equaliser on the stroke of full-time. It was to be Groundhog Day as the same happened again, a fine strike by their pesky left back who cut inside and sent in an unstoppable shot into the top corner. As the whistle blew shortly after, several of our players sunk to their knees or held their heads in their hands. It was hard not to feel sorry for them as their commitment could not have been faulted and we'd been the better side throughout..

We made a swift exit and marched briskly back to the station to catch the train. We were accosted by a Carlisle fan bearing a remarkable resemblance to our one-toothed Cambridge fan. He was obviously chuffed to get a point, but I couldn't really take in what he was saying, and it's not easy to lip-read broad Cumbrian. Still he was friendly enough, much like most supporters in this League.

We were picked up by Michelle and Denise at Whitehaven station. It was a fairly short drive back to the hotel but it was suddenly punctuated by exclamations of "Oh my God". Michael and I were oblivious but the women explained that walking along the pavement were two blokes completely starkers, apparently looking like they were somehow shackled to each other. Two things occurred to me. First, if it was some sort of stag night prank it was pretty mean because it was by now sub-zero in temperature. Second, would Mike and I not have noticed anything were it two naked young women shackled together? The women had their own views as to the answer to the latter question.

We enjoyed a pleasantly relaxed dinner – certainly compared to the previous evening when we'd stuck a pin in the menu. The following morning we went our separate ways, and we took a very picturesque drive back through the Lake District, the Pennines and the Derbyshire Dales where we broke our journey back half-way. There was a snow covering everywhere and it made me realise that if you could trust the weather in the UK there really wouldn't be any need to go abroad for a holiday. But only if you can avoid the M6 in the process.

Next up Wycombe.

CHAPTER 11

WYCOMBE

Our Wycombe Wanderers tickets had already been purchased by the time we went to Carlisle and I was glad that our journey would be much shorter. I was even more glad I'd got tickets when, on the Tuesday in between the two games, we broke our winless home league run with an out of the blue 6 second half goals against York. Admittedly, York had been a poor side – destined to go out of the league I suspected unless they had a miraculous turnaround in fortunes and playing staff – and we were helped when they went down to 10 men just before half-time when Jonathan Greening (ex Man Utd as Howard from Guildford would no doubt tell you) was sent off. Nonetheless it suggested a possible change in our fortunes.

The morning after the York game, when I went into my work inbox,there were two e-mails, the first requiring my attendance at a training seminar about "unconscious bias"; the second requesting me to read our newly-published whistle-blowing policy. It got me wondering if referees have training on either of these subjects. In fact I wondered what training linesmen and referees have to undergo, say, at the start of each season. I imagined a League Two lineo toddling off for a day's refresher training pre-season and returning home to this sort of conversation with the wife:-

"What did you do at your training day today dear?"

"Well, first of all we did bleep tests for an hour – you know, just to make sure we haven't drunk too much sangria on holiday"

"Then, on the basis that we've not had to run sideways for the last 3 months, we had a running sideways assessment. They brought in this PT instructor and we had to do ring a ring o'roses for an hour. It doubled up as a bonding session."

"Before lunch we did gestures. You know, when a bloke runs back from an offside position to go for the ball in an onside position and the crowd howl when you put your flag up. We now have to do that hand gesture which demonstrates he's been offside when the ball was kicked. It's meant to make us more crowd-inclusive"

"Because we'd done all the physical stuff before lunch, we did more gestures after. We moved on to the "nodding slowly" training. Like when the full back fouls the winger and you wave your flag vigorously for the foul and the full-back starts spitting venom in your face in complete denial. I now have to nod my head slowly and calmly to demonstrate that I knew it was a free-kick and so did he. That was quite interesting actually. They brought the Churchill dog from the insurance advert in to do that. He told us to keep the nodding slow and smooth and to say "Yes, oh yes" in our heads while nodding."

"Finally we were tested on discipline. We had to completely ignore the ball rolling past us slowly and resist the temptation to kick the ball back to the bloke who's taking the throw. That's really hard"

Seriously, have you ever known a linesman move to kick the ball back to a player? Managers in the technical area do it, and occasionally so do referees, but when have you ever seen a linesman shift from playing musical statues as a ball rolls past him?

Anyway, and not wishing anyone to think that my mind wanders while I'm at work, back to Wycombe

High Wycombe is about an hour and a half in the car, longer if you travel by train and cross London. The train is also more expensive at a whopping £38 for a day return. I was a bit scarred by the M6 though, so opted for the train. I was going up with Paddy only for this game but we hoped to meet up with others inside or outside the ground.

We got on the train at Petersfield and it was half-full until Guildford when a number of pre- Christmas shoppers jumped on. I've moaned about SW Trains earlier but the fact is that on a relaxed and leisurely punctual journey there is nothing to beat travelling by train. On the hour stretch from Petersfield to London we were able to look out over some of the best golf courses in Surrey, Sandown Park racecourse and a host of sprawling houses that you can't even begin to see from the road, and passing through South West London the Oval, the Shard and the London Eye successively come into view.

Arriving at Waterloo, we scooted across to Marylebone on the underground. I know that lots of Londoners moan about it, but how can anyone complain about a transport service where you can cross one of the world's biggest capital cities in such short time and where even if you miss one train you only have to wait a couple of minutes before another one turns up.

With time to spare before our connection to High Wycombe we grabbed a coffee and emerged from the station to have a smoke outside. There we encountered one of London's unsung worthies – a bloke on the job emptying the bins outside the station, carefully separating the recyclable from the non-recyclable. I couldn't hear all that he was saying to the crowd standing around the smoking area, but he muttered about idiots that put the wrong kind of plastic in the recycling bin, and regaled us with the history of his day's work, detailing how many bins he'd so far emptied and how many more he'd visit before he finished his shift. It reminded me of Trigger and his broom stick how intent he was on making sure that his job was done quickly and efficiently, and although it would be easy to take the piss, in some ways it was reassuring that some people could take pride in what others might see as the most mundane daily routine. I was so impressed by his dedication that I was too guilty to deposit my butt anywhere near his recently cleared bin, so walked about 20 yards to the nearest drain.

The train from Marylebone to Wycombe was just two carriages long but it whizzed through West London at a rate of knots. Yet again there are things you can observe from a train window that you can't see from the road and on this stretch of rail it was the number of urban gardens which had been partially set aside to vegetable plots.

We arrived at Wycombe just before one, and exited the station 20 yards ahead of a group of lads in Pompey shirts who started chanting "Blue Army" as soon as they were outside the train. Now Paddy would say I'm an old fart but I can't say I'm comfortable with people chanting their team's songs anywhere other than a football ground. Maybe in a designated away pub or just outside the ground, but not in a town centre 3 miles away from where the game is taking place, amongst shoppers and others who probably have no interest, even knowledge, of a football match taking place at 3pm that day. It just seems a bit yobbish to me.

We were due to meet Chop and Toni who'd travelled up by car, but had no text to say they'd arrived so slipped into The Bootlegger, closest bar to the station, which had a fantastic range of real ales and bottled beers. We were only able to sample one until we were summoned by Toni's text, to the realities of The Falcon, a Wetherspoons pub in the High Street, where we were eventually served a couple of beers amidst the crowd at the bar being served by a woefully inadequate number of staff. We eventually found Chop and Toni who were sitting at a table with Belinda and Brad who'd also made the trip separately. By now it was gone 2 and we finished our drinks and gratefully accepted Brad's offer of a lift rather than summoning a taxi. His satnav took him down some back streets which ran parallel to the main road and we slalomed through parked up roads to eventually park on a verge which still left us a three- quarters of a mile walk to the ground, which is situated at the far edge of High Wycombe, at the end of an industrial estate.

By now Paddy was wishing he'd visited the Wetherspoons little boys room and as we walked to the ground he constantly whinged that his bladder was at bursting point. As we got to the ground I saw his chin drop as he saw the queue for the away end which was moving slowly towards the gate as everybody was being frisked and searched by the stewards. We joined the queue and the people around us must have heard his intermittent low groans.

I've never quite understood why everyone is searched before entering a sports stadium. You don't have to open your handbag if you're a woman going to the pictures or the theatre, but even my 78 year old Mum has to open her bag at Pompey home games, though the only thing they would ever find is boiled sweets for sharing with the various OAPs sitting around her, and perhaps a few arthritis tablets. It just seems to me to be a lot of going through the motions to tick a box.

Equally, if stewards and police have to do a job like this it helps enormously that they do it with a laugh and a joke. Being only 30 miles or so from Oxford, the policing and stewarding was nonetheless so much more relaxed to the extent that the bloke in front of me even proposed marriage to the middle aged female steward who'd invited him to join the queue. Not the queue to marry her, she wasn't unduly attractive, I mean the queue for the ground.

Eventually getting inside the away end, Paddy ran to the gents in a world record time whilst I queued up for the pies which proved to be nothing more than average.

The away fans were allocated a whole end and we were sited about half way up just to the right of the goal. This was called the Dreams stand, presumably because it was sponsored at some stage by the bed people, and I hoped that the game would be such that I wouldn't yearn for one of their products. The home end was covered terracing whilst the stand to our left was the most impressive and set aside for home supporters. The stand to our right was less impressive but because the demand for tickets was greater than the Dreams stand could accommodate, part of that stand was occupied by away fans, including Chop and Toni who'd bought their tickets at the last minute. In some respects it was like a larger version of Cheltenham in that from where I was sitting, I looked out over open fields and woods. The similarities between Cheltenham and High Wycombe end there however because Cheltenham as a town has all the style that Wycombe rather surprisingly lacks bearing in mind it is in close proximity to London and presumably in the Buckinghamshire commuter belt.

Wycombe were just inside the play-off spots so we expected a tough game, but within a few minutes it became clear that the task ahead would be even tougher. Though we had pretty much a first choice team out, we lacked our usual passing fluency as we were closed down quickly by the home side.

About half-way through the first half, disaster struck. A through ball would almost certainly have been comfortably dealt with by our centre-back Christian Burgess but in a moment of poor decision making that was becoming just a little too regular our 'keeper Brian Murphy decided he'd play rush goalie. Fifteen yards outside his box, the clearance was poor and the ball found its way to a Wycombe player on the edge of the centre circle who simply had to implement his practice for the Crossbar Challenge as he returned the ball with interest into an empty net, Murphy returning to his goal in a slower time than Paddy's rush to the Wycombe bogs before the game.

It wasn't the first error from Murphy in the season and there were some howls of derision towards him from the away end. Matters took a turn for the worse about five minutes later as a flowing Wycombe move on the break saw a delicious cross come in from the right which was belted home at the far post.

And it was then that the fight started.

I hadn't taken much notice of the people around me but Paddy clearly had. I was seated to his right and to my right there were three lads about his age. Directly in front of me were three guys about my age. They didn't have the appearance of anything other than normality. The bloke in the middle had ginger hair and glasses and was wearing something which looked suspiciously like a yellow oilskin jacket. His mate to his right was pretty innocuous in appearance and the fellow to his left was grey haired, somewhat rotund and about five foot four. Immediately after the second goal went in, the two older guys on the right immediately below us turned round and started throwing punches at two of the three younger lads to my right. I'd no idea what had prompted this but I nudged Paddy and we stood watching this exchange of handbags somewhat bemused. There were a couple of pensioners behind me and they were pointing out the incident to a fellow pensioner who was acting as a steward and standing behind the goal. He returned their urgent gestures with a smile which suggested he'd seen the fight and was just going to let them get on with it.

Suddenly, the squat older guy in front completely out of the blue swung a haymaker at the third lad, standing immediately to my right. He missed by a mile but by now Paddy had seen enough and told the ageing pugilist to leave it out as the lad hadn't been doing anything. It all sort of calmed down though there was still a bit of pointing. The wannabe fisherman was muttering about decking the lad he'd traded blows with though there didn't seem much likelihood of that. None of them looked like they'd done 30 seconds with Mike Tyson, more like they'd had a dance with Audley Harrison on Strictly.

The game resumed and in a rare breakaway just before half time, Mark McNulty sprung the offside trap and squared unselfishly for Caolan Laverty to tap home. The rival gangs below and alongside us congratulated each other a little coolly about our now expected comeback. Going in at half-time only 2-1 down flattered us. It was the only time I'd seen us outplayed this season, apart from maybe a few short spells at Oxford.

Over the half-time interval Paddy explained the build-up to the rumpus after the second goal. It appeared that the young lads had been joining in the song about "Wycombe's a shithole I wanna go home" and the ginger bloke had turned round and told them to "F...off home then". The undercurrent had escalated from there onwards, no doubt the tension rising after our poor showing on the pitch. I noted however that at half-time cordiality resumed and the confrontational atmosphere between the two groups had evaporated

It all changed after half-time on the pitch as well. We came out sharper and our passing was crisper. Not long into the half we equalised when Adam Webster scored with a near post header to increase our rather sketchy goals to corners seasonal ratio.

The equaliser was the cue for a love in between the two rival adjacent armies, who celebrated triumphantly together with arms around each other. I remarked to Paddy that if we got the winner we could be looking at full-blown shagging.

For the rest of the game we were on top, pressing for the winner. The crowd chanted "3-2, we're going to win 3-2" the chant actually being conducted by the OAP steward who was by now sitting on a stool behind the goal and facing the away end. He also put his fingers up in a 3-2 gesture by way of his concurrence that an away winner was on the way.

It didn't come but we should have been awarded a penalty. We had several corners and the defenders were becoming increasingly tactile in manhandling our players as they tried to attack the ball. At one corner Christian Burgess was effectively dragged to the ground by his marker as he tried to make his run. 2,350 fans screamed for what was a stonewall penalty but the referee, standing virtually on top of the incident, ignored it completely and pointed for a goal kick.

I really don't understand this development in football. From the Premier League through League Two a gentle pull-back or shirt tug in the centre circle results in a certain yellow card but a referee will turn a blind eye to a defender performing the Heimlich manoeuvre on an attacker at a corner or set piece. Seems to me that it would be simple to eradicate it – just go in the changing rooms before the game and tell both sets of players that manhandling or even obstruction in these situations will mean penalties and yellow cards. It would soon stop.

The game fizzled out to what was a fair 2-2 draw. Not wishing to miss the bus back to the Town, whose post-match location I'd established from a steward, I nonetheless paid a quick trip to the gents on the way out. It was then that I realised that Wycombe must have the smallest toilets per capita in the football league. It was like standing in the queue for the portaloos at Glastonbury or before the Great South run. Neither could the plumbing cope. By the time I'd performed the necessary, I must have smelled like an inmate at the country's worst Nursing Home.

The delay in performing this natural function meant that upon walking to the end of the industrial estate where I'd been told I'd find the Bus Special it had either gone or it had been a mirage in the first place. So Paddy and I started the long walk back to town as the rain started to come down and an hour later, and pretty soaked, we reached the entrance to The Bootleggers which we decided to sample once again. We were just in time to see Jamie Vardy equal the Premier League consecutive scoring record on the televised evening game, and stood at the bar chatting with a couple of Blackpool fans, father and son.

The older of the two was clearly a long-standing supporter who didn't go to any of their home games out of protest against the Oystons, but went virtually everywhere away. We compared our respective demises and debated whether it was worse to have no money and go bust or to have surplus cash but invest it in the owner's pockets rather than the club. It was a bit like one of those "I had it worse; I lived in a shoebox in the road" conversations, but we passed a pleasant half-hour with them before effecting our egress to the station, where frustratingly, we arrived just in time to see the train arrive on the platform and start to move away just after we'd run over the bridge to jump on. I resisted the urge to go Die Hard and jump on the roof, reserving my ire for the driver who I'm sure I saw doing a "yah boo sucks" gesture in his wing mirror.

Fortunately the trains from Birmingham to Marylebone, last stop Wycombe, were pretty frequent and we only had to wait half an hour for another. Although busy, we managed to find seats opposite a pretty young girl in her early twenties, on her own, who'd got on the train at the same time.

There was a group of Pompey stragglers, like us, who were stood up by the doors at the end of the carriage. They had obviously been chatting with the girl on the platform, because periodically the words "I love you Lauren" and "Lauren, will you marry me?" were called down the carriage. The poor girl looked on the one hand flattered but on the other flustered as she played with her 'phone, muttering to the people next to her that she wished she hadn't told them her name. As we approached Marylebone, one of them called down "Lauren, only a minute to tell me you love me", before the train hit the buffers and she made a red-faced exit. Some would call it harmless fun, others harassment, but while she looked a little embarrassed she didn't show any sign of being intimidated, because had she looked like she felt like she was being anything worse than teased, I think someone would have asked the lads to cut it out. Perhaps Lauren was just a High Wycombe variety of the moosh-bird.

A scamper on the Tube across London, a quick visit to the tuck shop and hopping on the fast train back, we arrived at Petersfield about 9. It had been a good day all round and we opted to have one for the road at the covered courtyard bar at Annie Jones. There we met James Gurney, one of elder son Danny's mates. Gurney knew I was writing about our Awaydays and asked if Danny had featured. I said not so far but we planned to do Accrington together after Christmas and he said that a decent group of them were going to the same game. Like a true friend he suggested that when writing about Accrington I should just refer to Danny throughout as "the middle child". I just said I'd think about it and we took our leave.

CHAPTER 12

A MID-SEASON LULL

I hadn't planned on doing either of our two away games in December. On the Saturday before Christmas we were at Northampton who had gone on a run of wins and were now heading the table; on Boxing Day we were away at Leyton Orient, but it's rare that I ever get to an away game over Christmas, and I'd been to both grounds before. Leyton Orient's ground is situated in built up east London and there's a block of flats which overlooks one corner of the ground. The last time I'd been there it had prompted the chant "we can see you, we can see you, we can see you washing up"

December started with us home to Accrington in the FA Cup. I managed to hook up with a hospitality table at Fratton for the princely sum of £35 including the match ticket. We won 1-0 with an Adam McGurk goal and were in the hat for the 3rd round. Unfortunately this was to be played on 9th January when our scheduled League Two game had been away to Morecambe, and I'd planned to take in that game and the game on 16th January nearly as far north, at Accrington. The Morecambe game would now be re-arranged for a midweek night which made it really difficult.

A resounding home win against Hartlepool was followed by a 2-1 away win at Northampton which put us back in touch with the three automatic promotion places after our run of draws in November, but our Christmas games produced a 3-2 defeat at Leyton Orient after Adam Webster had been slightly harshly sent off, and a disappointing 0-0 draw at home to Luton, now managed on a caretaker basis by Andy Awford following the sacking of John Still.

The Luton game produced some amusing moments, mind. Never the best of friends the two sets of supporters nonetheless engaged in some quite humorous banter. Half way through the first half we won a free-kick just outside the box and Ben Davies curled his shot round the wall and just outside the post into the side netting. The home fans stood up for a moment but then collectively sat down and groaned, frustrated. The stadium announcer, however, broadcasted that the scorer of the Pompey goal was Ben Davies, puzzling as every player was just trotting back into position for the goal kick.

Cue the whole of the Fratton End leaping around as if we had scored after all. It didn't stop there. A minute later, as a Luton shot cleared the bar by about 20 yards they too jumped up and celebrated collectively. It happened at both ends for the rest of the half every time an attempt on goal was missed, interspersed with chants of "Sacked in the morning" directed towards the stadium announcer. Stuff like this is why I love live football.

We got back on track with a 3-0 home win against Crawley before the year ended but Plymouth, Northampton and Oxford were all winning at will and we once again slipped a few points behind the automatic spots.

The Christmas period had also thrown up a TV programme which I was keen to see; a Christmas celebrity version of Mr and Mrs in which Harry Redknapp and his wife Sandra were to be one of the couples. I wanted to see the programme for a variety of reasons. Firstly to try to get a feel for the Harry

Redknapp persona outside a football setting. Secondly to see what sort of questions they would give him and Sandra to answer; and finally to see the mystical Sandra for the first time.

Sandra had been mentioned by Harry in post match interviews for as long as I could remember. Who was this woman with whom Harry would habitually but quietly celebrate an unexpected win over "a plate of pasta and a glass of red wine" and whose apparent ability to have notched the far-post header, which Darren Bent had so famously missed against us after Harry moved on to Tottenham, had been highlighted in Harry's post-match interview? As it happened, the third question was fairly quickly apparent. Sandra seemed pretty normal in a lot of ways, clearly tolerating Harry happily but seemingly without any inherent affection towards football. She certainly didn't come over as the 1960s equivalent of an empty-headed WAG.

The second question was answered by some disappointingly mundane questions about Harry's DIY skills, what he'd turn off the television and similar topics. I was disappointed by this, having rather expected something like:-

"Sandra, which of these is Harry's favourite day of the year:-

A. His birthday
B. Christmas Day
C. Transfer Deadline day"

Or perhaps:-

"Harry, how does the Redknapp turkey look on Boxing Day:-

A. Still plump and juicy
B. Enough left for cold sandwiches
C. Down to bare bones."

And when he answered his questions, I couldn't wait to hear him say "oh – for sure, it's number 3."

Anyway, I was sorely disappointed by the lack of imagination in the questions.

Finally, how did Harry come over in a non-football setting? To my mind as I'd expected, largely normal despite his obvious surplus of cash, but also mirroring his "cheeky chappie Cockney" image. I could imagine him hurling his 7-iron when he heard that we'd been drawn away to Man Utd in the Cup quarter final in 2008, but imagined that he would also be a good man manager to match his apparently quick temper.

Nobody, but nobody, divides the Portsmouth fanbase as much as Harry Redknapp .Chop and Steve are pretty virulently anti, Andy and I have more ambivalent views. I don't think any Pompey fan would say that they loved Harry Redknapp even after he came back and pulled off our great escape. Taking the job at Southampton after he fell out with Milan Mandaric had been to nearly everyone an act which looked to have been borne out of some sort of revenge. Mind, he never looked happy or comfortable in that role, no-one who saw the press conference on his first day down the road, when he looked so uncomfortable holding up a Southampton scarf, really thought that he felt himself that it was a sensible move.

What I don't understand is this retrospective self-righteousness, now that we are a goody two shoes largely fan-owned club (and as a full Trust member I think I'm entitled to a view on this) that Harry Redknapp was at fault for our financial demise. If I go to my CEO and say that I'd like to recruit a few big-hitters to my team, I expect him to ask me for a cost/benefit projection. Seems to me that our financial managers should have done the same to Harry when he came knocking to buy a few players. If my CEO doesn't ask me searching questions, am I really going to voluntarily point out potential pitfalls or just take on the expensively paid staff? If it makes my job easier then surely any normal person would take the latter option.

The fact is that Harry's management gave Portsmouth its most successful modern era. It's very easy to forget that he transformed a team which had nearly been relegated in 2001 to one which seemed virtually invincible the following season, doing so with a mix of clever loans and some really astute signings at pretty modest cost, players like Matty Taylor and Toddy. Granted, players like Merson, Tim Sherwood and Stevie Stone (my favourite of all Pompey players in the Redknapp era) didn't come cheap in terms of wages but there are plenty of managers who've used the sort of budget Harry was given by Milan Mandaric and failed miserably. Harry bought a few numpties along the way but even after we were promoted to the Premier League he still pulled a few rabbits out the hat like Arjan de Zeeuw who was languishing on the fringes at Wigan, Teddy Sheringham near the end of his career and Patrick Berger. He also started Gary O'Neil's career and recognised Linvoy's rejuvenation, reserve team regular transformed into perennial cult Pompey hero. In addition, he had a pretty good turnaround record in terms of cost of purchases and the subsequent sell-ons of the same players.

Sorry, but those are the times I remember, and for many the promotion season was the best we'd ever experienced. I don't accept that our budget was dramatically different to any others at that time, he just used it well. Unfortunately, he'll be remembered for his defection down the road and our subsequent descent into administration, but in between I doubt if any of the current donaters of Redknapp vitriol refused to go to the 2008 Cup Final on a point of principle. It was pretty obvious that it wasn't our capacity gates that were funding the wages of people like Sol Campbell, but I wonder if Bournemouth fans are realising that the same applies to them, and even Chelsea fans, despite their commercial income.

And as for those self-righteous opinions from other clubs' fans, just remember there but for the grace go you. There are a few clubs like West Brom and Arsenal who are run on a sound financial footing, but most are kept afloat from their over-spending by Sugar Daddys (or Mummys in the case of them nearby in red and white stripes). Just make sure that they don't get bored and their bank backers don't become as trigger-happy as ours were.

At least in the lower divisions, living beyond means is a virtual impossibility. We're lucky enough this season to be able to afford to pay a bit more because we have a bigger fan base than everyone else and more people coming through the turnstiles. It will be a bit different if and when we get back to the Championship.

But with an eye to the past, back to the present. The 3rd round draw pitted us away to Ipswich, in a repeat of the start of our 2008 Cup-winning success. Strangely I'd not been to Portman Road and on the basis that I'd originally set aside the weekend for Morecambe, I persuaded the family to have a weekend away. I managed to get four tickets for me, Michelle, Nic and Paddy and we booked a couple of rooms in the Premier Inn down by the river. I was confident that we'd avoid defeat because of Michelle's lucky presence.

Setting off early on a mild Saturday morning we sailed through the Dartford Tunnel and on to the Ipswich road. On the way we'd rejuvenated our test of Nic's mooshbird status by asking her to name all the football grounds in the League. She was virtually flawless until she got to League One but even Paddy and I struggled with the likes of Burton. Michelle was bored by this conversation and started clacking her knitting needles in the back of the car but chipped in with a few perlers when given a cryptic clue. The most amusing moment was passing Colchester's ground which I remembered as Layer Road. It had now moved out of town and was known as the Weston Homes Community Stadium, impossible not to tag because it was plastered all over the stand facing the road, and which I pointed out. The fact that just 10 minutes later Nic could not name Colchester's ground gave rise to some ridicule. It also gave rise to the question of what does Colchester have which is the biggest in the country. Paddy gave a few crude answers involving certain private parts for which he was reprimanded by his unimpressed mother, but no-one got the answer – its railway platform. I'm sure Andy would have known assuming the answer is actually correct

Unable to check in to the hotel, we parked up and strolled along the river aiming to get a bite to eat. It was curiously devoid of much activity but we walked a bit closer to the ground and found a leisure retail park with the usual suspects and plumped for a Maccy D, which is somewhere I only ever visit if on a motorway or before a football match. It satisfies my only very occasional craving for fast food.

We'd arranged to hook up with Andy and Steve at a pub just the other side of the river, opposite the station, which was quite close to the ground and pretty much given over to away fans. They had taken a detour to pick up Alf, another of our back of the Fratton stand half- time pundits, who lived in East Anglia.

A couple of pints later after a seemingly endless queue at the bar we walked to the ground which is located in the town itself. Back in the 70s I remember – in those days when football was often played on mud like at Derby's Baseball Ground – that this was what Pompey and Ipswich reputedly had in common, namely the best two pitches in the Football League.

Having been to a few newer lower league grounds now like Crawley, Oxford and Wycombe, and indeed a few higher up the League, it was good to go to a ground in the town centre like Portman Road. To my mind a football ground should be in the centre of a city, not in an industrial park, and it should always be close to a railway station. There is a lot of debate in Portsmouth about one day moving to a new ground but I'd personally vote to stay where we are but make the absolute best of what we've got by revamp and improvement. A football ground is part of the soul of a city. Wherever you go in Newcastle city centre, St. James's Park sits proudly in view and I think that's the way it should be in all great football cities. Stuff the extra capacity and income if the result is an IKEA flatpack .

Inside the ground it was equally as appealing. True, all of the atmosphere came from the away fans but I could imagine that full and raucous, it was a great place to be in the Ramsey days or the Bobby Robson managerial era, especially on European nights. A curiosity was the number of mascots Ipswich seemed to have, a seemingly endless parade of different furry creatures none of whom seemed to give any great insight into Ipswich's alter ego. Admittedly, it isn't easy to create a mascot out of a tractor but this just looked like an episode of the Banana Splits.

I also warmed to it because it gave me the best 90 minutes of football I'd seen from Pompey this season. Admittedly it was against a League One team with a number of second-string players, but remember that our team had been put together from fringe Championship and League One players. We played football and they played hoofball, a neutral would have thought that we were the Championship team. The first half ended 0-0 but the stats showed we'd had 72% possession, higher than we'd achieved at any other game this season. It was great to watch. Even better when we equalised through Kyle Bennett after Ipswich took the lead in the second half, even better still when Conor Chaplin scored again just minutes after coming on as sub. I missed Ipswich's fortunate equaliser with just minutes left because I'd been arguing with Paddy about how many minutes we thought the referee would add on. When I saw the goal later it looked a real softie and could be put down to goalkeeping error, though there was a strong argument that Brian Murphy had been fouled as he let a fairly harmless free –kick from the left flank drift over him into the corner of the net. We trooped away from the ground in some ways pleased with the result but in others deflated that we'd been so dominant yet had not won first time round; but a replay at Fratton would no doubt be well attended to swell the coffers a tad more.

Nic had arranged to meet some friends (who'd moved from Portsmouth back up to Ipswich) under the Alf Ramsey statue and we enjoyed a drink with them before getting a taxi back to our hotel, emerging later only to have a look around Ipswich and grab a bite to eat. We ended up in a half-empty pub to eat pretty standard pub grub. Walking back to our hotel, Ipswich seemed to be a pretty run down sort of place to me. One thing England had done really well in my opinion was to spruce up its' waterfronts, riversides and canalsides, from Liverpool to Newcastle, Bristol, Nottingham and even to Portsmouth. Ipswich just seemed 20 years behind, with lots of potential but very little investment to develop its' riverside tenements and warehouses. There were some signs that it was beginning to happen but overall it was unexpectedly dreary. Eddie Shoestring must be turning in his grave.

The following Saturday had long been earmarked for the away game at Accrington and it would be my first away outing this season with the middle child. Danny had got the Saturday off work and he got us both added to a big group which was going to the game under a loose package organised by Stuart Wallis who was manager of the Clanfield Hampshire League side and whose day job involved organising, with his business partner Malc, sports related events and tours such as those which we used to go to at Butlins in Minehead.

The party was going to be a mixed group; a number of Danny's mates; some older Pompey diehards; and some of Malc's old mates from Bolton. The plan was to get to our designated hotel – the Holiday Inn in central Bolton – about late morning, then get a pre-arranged coach to Accrington where we would enjoy a hospitality package the likes of which only League Two can offer and at a price to match.

Much as I was looking forward to the weekend, I was also apprehensive for a couple of reasons. The first was that we would be going to The Wham Stadium. In my mind Accrington Stanley always had a mystical history. I remember, when I was about seven, getting for Christmas a book called "A Pictorial History of Soccer". One of the pictures was of Accrington Stanley's old stadium derelict following their financial demise in the mid-60s with tumbleweed floating amongst the terraces. The fact that they had later reformed from the ashes and gradually climbed back to the football league's main divisions was a wonderful achievement. It seemed to me sad that it had been defaced by having its' stadium renamed The Wham Stadium, presumably taking the name of its' sponsor. Why do sponsors inflict such humiliation? Surely it should be enough to rename a stand for a couple of years at most, particularly if you're called Wham.

The second reason was that I'd be spending the weekend in the company of Danny's mates. Not that they aren't a good bunch of lads, more that these boys can really knock stuff back on a day or night out and I was concerned what state I'd be in at the end of the day. Also, they weren't known to each other by their first names in most cases. There were so many of them on their Whats App group that there were several Dannys, Jacks and James such that they referred to each other instead by their surnames. So instead of James and Jack we had Cooper and Gurney and there was also Potter (genuinely Harry Potter, he'd once appeared in The Sun bemoaning his moniker which had been given to him before Voldemort was a twinkling in JK Rowling's vivid imagination.).

Fifty years ago my young brain had taken a year to master the Trumpton firemens' names of Pugh, Drew, Barney McGrew, Cuthbert, Dibble and Grubb. Fifty years on, with brain cells disintegrating the other way, I had to do a similar thing all over again.

Accrington had a few games in hand on the teams above us, including us, as a result of the floods in the North-West. Whilst not as badly hit as Carlisle, they'd hardly played a home game since last Christmas, well mid-November anyway. But it had been a dry week which had got increasingly colder so we were confident, as was the Accrington website, that the game would go ahead.

Being the designated driver for the weekend as between me and Danny, I decided on an early night on the Friday. We'd have an early start in the morning and I didn't trust the M6 to be traffic free. As I mounted the stairs, Danny shouted up "wake me up before you go-go." Which I did at about 6 am on the Saturday morning.

It was a cold crisp day with a heavy frost on the windscreen when we left but the road was pretty clear and we decided to stop off at Warwick services for a coffee. There in the car park we came across the other lads being driven by Wallis, namely Potter, Gurney, Cooper and Calvin (presumably not Linkhorn because there weren't any other Calvins). The well of the back of the car was already five deep with beer bottles and I decided that these were bad boys.

We said we'd see them later and bombed past Birmingham on to the M6 which was mercifully free-flowing for once. We talked about the game ahead and our likely line-up. I wondered if Cook would play the young guns and go for it. In the week before the game Gary Roberts, back from injury, had proclaimed "I'm your man" and we thought that perhaps the

141

manager would prefer the older heads and let them play with more freedom. Either way, I hoped that the end result would mean that I was on the edge of heaven.

Just short of Sandbach services Danny insisted that he could wait no longer for a Maccy Ds breakfast and making such good time I felt we could afford to stop again. But worrying messages were coming through on his Whats App group suggesting there was going to be a pitch inspection at 10 a.m. It could only be because of frost which seemed to have got thicker as we'd got further north. Nonetheless I ventured to suggest that these were just careless whispers.

Irritating as it was that the game had been called off it also posed a conundrum. Did we turn back and write off the cost of the coach and the hotel. And if not, did we find another game to go to or do something else. Looking at the fixtures, Blackburn were at home, as were a couple of the other clubs around Manchester like Bury. I even wondered if anyone might fancy the extra 50 miles to Morecambe which I'd originally expected to be doing the weekend before. My vote would have been for Blackburn I think, having not been to Ewood Park. Blackburn always made me think of a bloke I met once on a holiday in sunnier parts. While we were outside a bar drinking cocktails he was in and out of the bar watching the Man United game on TV. They'd gone from an unexpected 2-0 down against someone like Norwich or Watford, to win 3-2 in the last five minutes. As he crooned at the victory, I commented that he didn't sound like he came from Manchester. He replied "No, I don't, I come from Gillingham but my family originate from Blackburn" Oh, that's close enough then but it does beg a question..........

The last of Danny's mates who was going to the game was Ash and he was getting an awful lot of mobile phone grief. He'd been at a Company function in Milton Keynes the night before and was coming up to Accrington by train. This apparently involved three changes and he was seriously pissed off.

As we got closer to Bolton there was a sign for the Macron stadium and I couldn't for the life of me think who played there. It wasn't Bolton because they played at the Reebok, which we'd all concurred upon in the car to Ipswich the week before. It was only later, when I asked one of the Bolton lads that I discovered that it was now the name of Bolton's ground. Presumably Reebok decided that they didn't want to be associated with Bolton after they slipped out of the Premiership. Still, at least they didn't get into bed with Wham.

We parked up at the hotel, and being unable to check in yet, I hovered around in reception while Danny established the plan. He came back to say that nobody fancied a game that didn't involve Pompey, so we were going on a motorised pub crawl in the environs of Bolton. This was turning into my potentially worst nightmare. It was by now only 11.30 a.m as I climbed on the coach and 20 minutes later when it stopped on the outskirts of Bolton at The Flag.

Fearing a row of pumps featuring lager from every part of the world, but no ale, I was pleasantly surprised to see that it could have been a one-pub real ale festival. Starting conservatively on the lowest APV beer on pump, I watched England skittle out South Africa for the sort of score that we used to consider a successful innings against the West Indies attack of Holding, Roberts and Garner in the 1970s. Like more than 50 but less than 100.

I also looked at the beams at the bar and saw that they were covered in plaques with peoples' names, though the names sounded like underworld criminals such as Smudger Mad Dog Smith and Billy "bonkers "Maloney. I asked the women behind the bar what this was all about and learned that they had all earned their plaque by going through 8 different pumps at the bar, the last of which had to be an 8 % cider which had to be finished in 8 seconds. As I walked further round the pub I was impressed that numerous women had completed this challenge and surmised that Bolton must have its' fair share of Mooshbirds.

After a couple of pints of superb hoppy beer, it was time to move on and we climbed back on to the coach, which was now going to take us somewhere more rural. Not having been to this part of the North-West before, I was surprised that there was anything other than an endless housing conurbation and it was therefore a pleasant surprise that less than 5 miles outside Bolton we were suddenly in the midst of bleak, albeit not yet wild, moorland which comprised the western edge of the Pennines. We passed through a village called Turton Bottoms which prompted me to text Andy. When we were at school our French teacher was called Miss Turton, who became known as Tits Turton as a result of her expansive chest measurements. Andy had been her little favourite – a fact which he acknowledged – so I felt that I had to tell him I was currently travelling through Turton Bottoms. He replied saying that he remembered her well. In fairness she was fairly sizeable all round. I remember one kid saying she was 36-24-36 and that was only round the left leg.

Next stop was The Chetham Arms, in a village called Chapeltown, where we tarried a short while and I was able to take in the view across the frost covered hills from the pub garden. This pub crawl was throwing up some surprises. Next stop was The White Horse at Edgworth, where the more sensible amongst us – being everyone over 30 – decided that before drinking any more beer, it was essential that we soaked it up with food.

While sitting at the bar eating home-made fishcakes, Danny and I got chatting to one of the locals, who knew Pompey well having been in the Navy. He'd lived in Portsmouth for a few years and he reminisced about his time down south, though strangely he confessed that he didn't know what we meant when we asked if he'd lived "on the island". With landfill it was of course easy to forget that Portsea is actually not naturally connected to other land. I knew this from my early years fishing off Portsbridge before the Hilsea roundabout was built.

I glanced along the bar, and spotted Potter drinking what looked suspiciously like Babycham. He claimed it was Prosecco and I began to take the piss. We got chatting about ladies drinks from the 60s and I regaled him with tales of women having their hair blue rinsed on a Saturday night ready for a night out at the social club where they'd indulge in Babycham, Cherry B and Snowball. I didn't think these drinks existed any more but if I saw a Babycham anywhere I'd buy him one to sample. I mean, it's one thing moving onto bottles of Sol or Desperado on a lengthy pub crawl, but Prosecco......

By the time we left the Edgworth Arms it was about 3.30pm. The Bolton contingent were cursing that they had gone 2-0 down to Forest inside the first 10 minutes, and their 'keeper had been sent off in the process. They were very much in the same financial position we'd been in a couple of years earlier and were talking about fledgling moves towards a takeover by the Supporters Trust.

And then it started snowing. We stood on the veranda outside the pub and the sight of snow laying on the hills to our left was the sort of sight I had not expected to enjoy on a pub crawl around Bolton. We lingered a short while before making our way back into Bolton, where our coach driver took his leave with a healthy tip and we settled in to watch the second half of Soccer Saturday.

I selected a pint of Costa del Salford ale – yes, correct, Costa del Salford – and we saw hopes rise as Plymouth went one down but then deflated as they went 2-1 up. As it happened we were going to have to take the points in what would be our game in hand at Accrington if we weren't to fall further adrift. And they in turn had games in hand on us.

The Ainsworth Arms was a pleasant enough pub on the outskirts of Bolton, but we'd been drinking beer now for the best part of 5 hours. I needed some mementoes of this pub crawl if I was to remember much of it, so got Danny to take a photo of me standing in the bar, with Timmy Mallet in the background. Truly, when I looked again at the photo the following day, I realised that I hadn't been so inebriated that I had tagged him correctly, he really was the spit of Timmy in looks and dress, even down to the hat.

After this much time on the town you also fall into philosophical (and usually inane) discussion but Danny, Gurney and I had a pretty intelligent debate about how we would like to see the England squad made up for the Euros this coming summer. I threw a few curveballs into the mix like Ryan Shawcross at centre back and ex-Pompey player Joel Ward, at Crystal Palace, as right back, where overall I thought he'd do as good a job as any of the more likely suspects at the bigger clubs. Possibly even Glen Johnson could come back into the frame and we could rejuvenate the "toilet seat at B and Q" ditty.

Jeff Stelling was by now looking exhausted after his quickfire delivery for the last 3 hours and we strolled a couple of hundred yards down the road to our penultimate venue, The Stork.

By now it had been snowing for 3 hours and there was a couple of inches laying so the walking proved a bit more cautious. But on arrival at this pub, which was on a terrace but whose clientele made me think of the Rovers Return, I spied the special offers behind the bar. Babycham £1.50, Snowballs £1.50, Cherry B £1.50. It was like going back in time. I swear I saw Rita Littleworth sitting at the bar. Ecstatic that I'd found Potter's Babycham I called him over and bought a round, insisting that he see it off before we left. He slugged half of it back like a shot but couldn't finish it off. Lightweight. You never saw Ena Sharples leave a drop.

There was one last pub to visit. It was called The Weaver Arms, and it was in the most out of the way location at the end of an industrial estate. I kept saying to Danny that we must be going the wrong way, but it suddenly loomed ahead through what was by now quite a heavy snowfall.

This pub had apparently once been the local of Wallis's business partner Malc so he wanted to visit it for nostalgic reasons. I suspect he may not be visiting it next year because it was pretty empty, there was no bitter on tap and it just seemed to be in its dying embers. I did however spend half an hour chatting to one of the Bolton contingent who was conducting some in-depth research into the Battle of Waterloo with a view to proving that an unsung and virtually unmentioned hero was responsible for the saving of the battle just as Napoleon looked to be breaking through. It's astonishing really that after seven hours in alehouses it was still possible to have a pretty intellectual conversation and I was on reflection later quite proud of myself that I was coherent enough to have contributed towards it.

But by now, I was full to the brim with beer and I needed an hour's nap. Danny ordered a taxi and we got back to check in to our hotel about 7.30. He was going to be out on the town much later than me so went into the shower, whilst I was going out again only for food, so crashed out to recharge batteries. I was woken by Gurney jumping on my bed at 9 o'clock. I roused myself to freshen up quickly and we went back into the Bolton night where we found a curry house called Laibaz. If you're ever in Bolton give it a try, the food was fantastic, washed down with a pint of Cobra.

It was time for me to depart, and a final drink in Yates's where I was prevailed upon to try a bottle of Desperado, which was named like I felt after a session of this magnitude. However, I was the designated driver the following day and felt that I shouldn't partake any further. Feeling that I hadn't been a party pooper, I then excused myself and surprised myself by finding the way back through the snow to our hotel, where I gratefully slumped in to bed to watch the last hour of Match of the Day.

I only know that Danny arrived back at the room about 4.30 because he couldn't get his key to work, and roused me from what had been deep slumber.

We were up and away from the hotel the following morning about 11.30. I met Potter out the front, he had his dancing shoes in an empty cardboard box which had originally contained Budweiser or something similar, and he was seeing off the last bottle having apparently not eaten or slept for about 24 hours.

I'd not got to the delights of the Wham Stadium then; but I'd survived the weekend without disgracing myself and for that I was grateful.

CHAPTER 13

YEOVIL

Milkins; Pack, Ley: Smith, Tindall, Harris: McCann, Pointer, Hiron, Kellard, Jennings.

This was the team I remember from the 1967/68 season. It was mercifully free of injuries for the best part of 6 months and for long periods was flying in the promotion spots of the old Division 2. I put numbers on the back of my Subbuteo Pompey so that I could recognise them as individuals. There was no specific Pompey Subbuteo team and I had to paint the blue socks red to match the Pompey kit. In my Subbuteo world they regularly handed out 6-0 thrashings to Brazil, who were my second favourite Subbuteo line-up, and the scorelines against Partick Thistle, who I bought because they played in attractive yellow and red hoops, were even more emphatic.

There are many people who believe that Pele, Jairzinho and Rivelino retired at various points in the 70s. I knew different. Their careers were actually ended by simultaneous double leg breaks incurred in the same game against Pompey in about 1973. They sustained these injuries following an argument with my sister about the singing capabilities of David Cassidy. It was an argument she could never win and in a fit of pique she inflicted career ending injuries upon three of the all time greats with the heel of her right platform shoe.

To say that I was heartbroken would be an understatement. Temporary rehabilitation was attempted with superglue but they were never quite the same, spinning left when they were meant to spin right. The defeats against my 67/68 Pompey team became heavier before I finally confined them to a box on the basis that games have to be abandoned if a team only has a certain number of players on the pitch.

This 67/68 Pompey team was much the same as the year previous but with the more regular addition of one of my favourite ever Pompey players, Ray Pointer. When he joined he gave us the equivalent of Cantona to Manchester United, or Suarez to Liverpool. He was a natural goalscorer, in a team which had a solid 10 goals a season from Ray Hiron and a few from Albie who actually ended up top scorer that year, Nicky Jennings and Bobby Kellard, not to mention the odd thunderbolt from Georgie Ley.

Ray Pointer had won the league with Burnley in the early 1960s . How romantic that a small town in Lancashire could win the English football League built on good scouting and a fantastic youth set-up – it just couldn't happen now amidst the big money boys of the Premier League – or could it, if Leicester kept defying the odds? Ray came to Portsmouth near the end of his career and scored goals for fun. We would surely have been promoted that year had Ray not broken his foot in early March, which ruled him out for the rest of the season. It was a defining week in our season in 1968. We'd enjoyed an exhilarating cup run including a narrow win against First division Fulham and then an exit at Fratton Park against West Brom in front of a huge crowd. I recalled most of this from memory but was helped by a scrapbook I still had, compiled as a result of an agreement with my Coventry City cousin that we'd both keep records of that season.

Thus it was that I was lying on my bed early in February tuned in to the Sky football special and the live Pompey text updates of our midweek game against Morecambe. I'd been banished upstairs as a result of Michelle wanting to watch "CSI Portsmouth; how to murder your husband without leaving any evidence" for about the twentieth time. Hmmmm.

Since the abortive weekend in Accrington, we'd won the FA Cup replay against Ipswich the following Tuesday with a really good team performance, setting us up for a gallant 4th round defeat against Bournemouth where we had dominated the game for long periods but succumbed to two late goals. In between, however, we had been outplayed in the league at home to Oxford in a promotion 6-pointer, and had lost 1-0 to fall further behind the automatic promotion spots. Our game in hand away at Morecambe, which had been re-scheduled from early January, offered the opportunity to get our promotion drive back on track.

We apparently dominated this game, and led from the first half, but could not score a second killer goal. I watched all the evening's matches, bar ours, show full-time and then suddenly, Stelling (and I was beginning to dislike him immensely) announced not only a last minute equaliser by Morecambe, but one scored by their goalkeeper who'd come up for a last minute corner. How could this happen? I recalled hundreds of occasions when goalkeepers had come up for last minute corners but never had I seen one score. I could only ever remember it happening once before when Jimmy Glass of Carlisle scored a late header to keep Carlisle in the league a few seasons back.

It seemed like a defining moment in our season, like the moment nearly 50 years earlier when Ray Pointer had broken his foot and our promotion hopes had fizzled out. It seemed particularly apt that it had happened just a fortnight after it was announced that Ray had died. I wondered if we could recover our season.

Just 5 days later we produced our worst performance of the

season to lose again against Orient in the home return fixture. They were no great shakes, but we'd played new signing Michael Smith as target man and he looked ring-rusty, and Kieron Freeman, a new loan signing from Sheffield United, at right back to give Ben Davies a mid-season rest. This game was notable for the fact that League two seemed to be carrying out an experiment in refereeing in that there were 5 officials on the pitch.; the referee, the two linesmen, the fourth official, and Kevin Nolan, the recently appointed Orient manager who seemed to make most of the decisions on the referee's behalf in typical Premier League fashion. Look, mate, if you're not good enough to play Premier League football any more, just retire because we don't want your sort polluting League Two. That said, despite Nolan refereeing the game, we'd looked half the team and fears were growing that not only were we way adrift of the top three, but we were also in a melee to retain a play-off spot. Last season's top League Two striker Matt Tubbs, who'd never seemed to be a Cook favourite, had been sent out on loan to Eastleigh and we were starting to wonder if Cook had lost the plot.

A first league win of the calendar year at home to Bristol Rovers, when we suddenly looked a decent side again, had rejuvenated the supporter's optimistic juices, but we needed a run of wins, starting at Yeovil, if we had any chance of catching Plymouth or Oxford, and even overtaking Accrington, who had games in hand on level points.

Yeovil was to be our hospitality game this season. It had cost a bit more than Cambridge the year before and we were expecting a high quality banquet with lashings of ginger beer in the words of Enid Blyton. The usual suspects were going; Chop, Andy, Steve and all the wives. There was precedent to suggest that we could come away with a resounding victory. Firstly, because we'd won so handsomely on our hospitality game last year. Secondly because Michelle was going and we never lost when she watched Pompey. Thirdly, because Yeovil were struggling to avoid demotion; and finally because Ryan Bird, who'd been at Cambridge last year, when we won 6-2, was now turning out for Yeovil.

We had two spare spots in our box and we persuaded Jim to make the trip. Jim is one of my Sunday morning 8-ball golf group, a man very set in his ways. He bases his social life around our annual golf holiday in May. He's 50 years old. His girlfriend Mette is about 10 years older than him but they've lived separately since about 1789. Mette has a daughter Vicky who has a couple of kids and Jim is the most devoted holistic granddad you'd ever wish to meet.

But he's eccentric. He'll drink 4 pints of lager on a night out but rarely less than 4 or more than 4. He has an aversion to driving. Mark, his best mate, will always pick him up for golf on a Sunday morning so he can have a couple of pints at lunchtime. He always plays darts on a Sunday night. He can wear his slippers and take his home 'phone into the pub garden next to his house because it's so close.

When we are away on or golf week, be it France, Turkey or Majorca, Jim will always want to get his PJs on after 4 pints. He'll rarely be in the mood for one of those sessions that become legendary; for Jim, they are a distraction to his routine.

So it therefore came as some surprise when just before we went to Yeovil, Jim announced that he'd bought a new car, a Nissan Leaf, being one of those cars which has to be charged up with electricity every 100 miles. I suggested that he might want to drive to Yeovil but he reckoned he'd have to drive it to somewhere like Warminster and charge it up overnight. His previous car had done about 10,000 miles in 5 years. If you were advertising it for sale, you would say that it had one lady driver. It had been sitting so long unused outside his house that mould had started growing around the windows. It was known in our golf group as "the Eden Project".

Jim had other peculiarities. He didn't own a TV so rigged up the most complicated system in his house whereby he could watch sport, in particular golf, by setting up his mobile 'phone in a way that he could project his Apps onto a screen in his house. It was a truly awesome operation to save the cost of a proper telly..

Jim always said that sex was over-rated and messy. He didn't eat breakfast, just rolled a fag. He had about 5 brothers and I remember him saying that he'd bumped into one of them, who lived just a couple of miles away, for the first time in about 5 years. He visited his mum in Wiltshire once a year. He was very proud of his post as Chairman of Governors at a school in Fareham and as Chairman of the Wallington village fete. Jim was known amongst us as the Mayor of Wallington.

We'd have debates about the English language. Jim was educated. We debated whether newspapers should use the word disgusting when discussing that a citizen's rights had been infringed; perhaps when Crystal or Chardonnay had been suspended from school for turning up with purple hair. Jim said that if this was anything, it was disgraceful; dog shit on the pavement was disgusting.

I have to say that I agreed with him on many things, most particularly the over-use of the word disgusting in the local press. We also both have a thing about poor spelling. There used to be a sign at Fratton Park which said that no liability was "excepted" for loss or damage caused whilst on the premises. In other words, the club accepted liability for any loss or damage. How can a business get such stuff wrong? To that extent, Jim and I were kindred spirits in that we agreed that infringements of basic rights was disgraceful but only dog shit on pavements was disgusting.

So it was that I picked Jim Andy and Bev up at Fareham for the Yeovil game. We bombed up to Yeovil in a couple of hours to hit our Premier Inn at about 11.30. I was longing to see a

"50 – animals in Road" sign so that I could take the mickey out of Bev, but there aren't any gantries on the A303. However the really bizarre thing was that there were actually 50 animals in the road. Dead animals, and to be precise dead badgers.

Twenty years ago I don't think I'd ever seen a badger, alive or dead. Twenty years on I don't think I've still seen one alive in the wild. But on the A303 they were lying prostate at the edge of the road, in the central reservation and in the road itself. I mooted with the others whether the Government had found a sneaky way to purge badgers rather than by an openly admitted cull, something which regularly attracted vitriol from the green lobby, who maintained that badgers were nothing to do with bovine TB, a fact upon which I am ill- qualified to pass judgement. However, I now wondered whether the night road closures were nothing to do with road improvement but instead an opportunity for minions at DEFRA to station kit-e-kat in the central reservations to entice badgers into an untimely roadkill death. This may be the result of a fertile imagination and watching too many films about CIA cover-ups. Alternatively, there just may be a proliferation of badgers near the A303.

Unusually, Andy made it all the way to Yeovil without needing a pit-stop. As we drove in to Yeovil, a rather unfortunate signpost caught the eye. It was to the crematorium, but the unfortunate bit was that underneath was a small parking symbol and directly under "Crematorium" the words "long stay". We wondered if anyone else had noticed how tasteless this made the combination on the signpost.

We were staying at the Premier Inn once again, this time for a comparatively extortionate £39 a room, but it was too early to check in so we asked the particularly helpful woman on reception if we could store our bags and walk next door into the Beefeater to buy our first beer. Chop, Toni, Steve and Sue were already there. Chop announced that he had been diagnosed with gout, that his feet were in agony, that he wasn't allowed anything containing wheat or hops and that accordingly he was on tap water; Steve had man-flu and was on the coffee. I went straight in for a pint of Butcombe bitter, conscious that Jim and Andy might prove my only drinking companions, with even Jim limited to 4 pints before PJ time.

We tarried half an hour and then caught taxis to the ground, Huish Park. This was named the same as the original ground with the sloping pitch but was about 3 miles outside the centre of town. On the way to the ground I made a momentous gaffe which was to come back to haunt me for the whole weekend. I asked whether anyone knew Yeovil's nickname and as expected Steve knew straight away that they were the "Glovers". We then got on to other nicknames in this division and thought of places like Northampton – the Cobblers, Wycombe – The Chairboys, and Luton – the Hatters. The conversation went on to what Pompey might have been called if our nickname wasn't Pompey and before brain engaged mouth I said "what about The Slappers?". There was a sharp intake of breath from the three women in the front row of our 7-seater and I wasn't allowed to forget it for the rest of the weekend and indeed beyond.

It's an interesting thought however as to why a small town like Yeovil should become known for making gloves, Northampton shoes, Luton hats, or Wycombe chairs. Did someone in trendy 19th century London suddenly say "I need some new gloves" and promptly take a Hansom cab on a 2 day journey down to Yeovil to stock up? Certainly, on our walk around Yeovil there was no evidence of a preponderance of leather goods shops (or indeed cows), just as I hadn't seen showrooms of fastidiously designed chairs while walking through High Wycombe, and in those days it wasn't as if you could just order online.

On arriving at the ground, we were directed to our hospitality box located at the back of the Tamburino stand.

It was really quite pleasant by League two standards, being a private box with a sliding patio door onto the stand below and designated seats immediately in front of the box. The marketing manager made us welcome and introduced us to our host for the day, a young girl who it turned out was very sweet but who perhaps needed a bit more training before being let out to exclusively host. For example, when she asked us for our drinks order it soon became apparent that she was unfamiliar with the subtle differences between lager, beer and cider which proved to be evident when the order turned up completely wrong. She was also asked what wine there was and her reply was quite simply "red or white" – and it was only as we were about to leave at the end of the day that we found what was quite a comprehensive wine list.

For all that we settled in quickly, and the food was ready pretty much straight away. Again somewhat bizarrely our hostess served up our chicken supreme and vegetables on plates which we soon realised were meant for the incredibly good chocolate torte dessert, which in turn looked pretty lost on the large dinner plates. We weren't too bothered by this because it was a simple operation to pile the plate up again for seconds.

Likewise, being a private box we could pretty much do what we wanted. It wasn't a particularly cold day but had it been, we could have got a pretty good view of the game from inside the box. Nobody took away our wine glasses 15 minutes before kick-off either.

This for me was a strange phenomenon about our football licensing laws. I'd been invited along to hospitality at that place the other side of the Hamble one afternoon and never one to pass up a freebie I'd ended up in a private box much like the one at Yeovil, albeit somewhat more modern and presumably at much greater cost. Fifteen minutes before the game our glasses of wine had been scooped away from us, as if we were naughty boys not to be trusted not to hurl the glasses towards the away supporters located further away than a world record javelin throw.

Having been to the Army-Navy rugby at Twickenham populated by squaddies and matelots who'd been drinking cases of beer since they got on their respective trains and coaches at 8 o'clock in the morning and who were still topping up throughout the game, in full view of the pitch, I wondered whether the distrust of the average football fan had now gone too far. I'm not suggesting beer nets next to seats like at the rugby, but there is something almost humiliating and presumptuous that a genuine football fan is unable to be trusted not to become unruly if allowed alcohol, for example, in a hospitality box.

In any event, lunch done and dusted we went outside our box to survey the ground and watch the players warming up. The end to our left was slowly filling up with Pompey supporters, fortunately for them it being a dry day, on what was an uncovered terrace. The stand opposite us was almost a mirror image of our stand less the hospitality boxes. It was while surveying this stand and more particularly the hoardings on the roof of the stand, that Jim and I noticed yet another unfortunate sign.

The seats on the opposite stand were in the main coloured yellow white and grey. In the corner of the stand however was a bank of about 6 rows of seats which were coloured black – as far as we could see, the only black seats in the stadium. The irony was that immediately above these seats was a hoarding proclaiming "Yeovil against racism". It just seemed somewhat avoidable to locate this sign above the only black seats in the stadium and we wondered if anyone had spotted this potential gaffe.

To our right was a covered terrace, again with advertising hoardings on the roof. One of them was for Folke Golf Centre and in quotation marks afterwards the strapline "where golf is supposed to be fun". I thought about this for only a couple of seconds before wondering what marketing expert had thought up this slogan. How many times had I played golf really badly and commented "and this is supposed to be fun?". In fact it had completely the wrong impact and Jim and I were in stitches at the ineptitude of the Folke Golf Centre's marketing advisors.

As kick-off time drew near we took up our seats at the back row of the stand. Surveying the demographics of the stand, there was a preponderance of over 50s supporters. One of them was ringing a bell on the minute every minute, though he was a far cry from John Westwood, being about 65 and not wearing Yeovil clown shoes. In some ways it's a puzzle to me why people bring musical instruments into a sports ground but I suppose it adds to the spirit of the occasion. In thinking back to when I first started going, there must have been a couple of thousand rattles cranking away at Fratton Park every game. I guess that rattles have just moved on to trumpets bells and drums.

We had a pretty strong side out at Yeovil, but they were on a bit of a roll after being rooted at the foot of the table for the early part of the season, and they got in our faces pretty quickly. Our passing game was interrupted and long balls were sent into the wide areas for lone striker Michael Smith to chase. He hadn't yet become a crowd favourite and despite his height he seemed to have an aversion to jumping for a header. In that respect he reminded me of Benjani who'd taken about 6 games to win a ball in the air. Hopefully Smith would prove as popular with the fans as Benjani ultimately became. At least he'd scored in one of his early appearances, something which was to elude Benji for a lot of games. I recalled that our original Benjani chant had been (to the tune of Volare) "Benjani o-o-o-o Benjani o-o-o-o; he comes from Zimbabwe, he's going to score today". When about 10 Saturdays passed and he hadn't, the chant changed (to the tune of Prince Charming) "Benjani, Benjani, score a goal there's nothing to be scared of". It made me realise how unoriginal our singing support had now become.

Smith seemed to be lacking support and we weren't helped when Gareth Evans limped off early in the first half, to be replaced by Ben Tollitt. He'd shown a few flashes when coming on as a sub on a couple of occasions and a number of fans I'd spoken to had thought he was worth a start. Unfortunately he didn't help his cause at Yeovil, giving the ball away far too often. Gary Roberts was also having one of those days where nothing was really coming off.

The first half seemed to end almost before it had started. There had been few if any chances either side. I toddled off to the hospitality gents where I bumped into Bill Albury, who I'd played golf with on many an occasion. Bill had played half a dozen games for Pompey in the early 60s and unbeknown to me until I'd been reading the programme before the game, had gone on to play nearly 400 times for Yeovil, being one of their most "capped" players. He was guest of honour at the game and was clearly making the most of the occasion.

Re-taking our seats for the second half, we saw our team start with what seemed like an upped tempo though our passing was poor and chances when they came were slightly more in Yeovil's favour. With about 15 minutes left they took the lead with a scrappy goal. As we edged towards the final whistle I said to Michelle that it looked like her unbeaten run was going to come to an end, but barely were the words out of my mouth than a Tollitt cross was volleyed home by Roberts with great technique. But there was no more excitement and the game ended 1-1. It hadn't been a showpiece.

We decamped back to our box for a post-game drink while awaiting for the traffic to clear. Like most out of town stadiums this took some time. It was akin to the stream of cars at the end of Field of Dreams. We got our drinks bill which was surprisingly modest and left a decent tip for the lovely but hapless hostess. Andy started ringing for taxis, which proved to be an unexpectedly difficult task. The plan had been to get back to our hotel, and have a leisurely relaxation period before emerging for the evening. It was not to be the case as it soon became apparent that taxis were few and far between in Yeovil, possibly because Radiotaxis, seemingly the biggest local company, had occupied the hospitality box next to ours. Alternative options were suggested but without success. Andy decided to go on a charm offensive. He ended his conversation with the next firm he rang with the somewhat robustly expressed words "what, are there only two taxis in Yeovil" and we gave up any hope of securing an early lift back to the hotel.

Chop had invited an ex-workmate, a Yeovil fan, into our box after the game and he suggested that we hike to a local pub and order our cab from there. Certainly, an hour after the game, the Marketing team at the football ground seemed to be keen to move us on before midnight, so we entered the evening air, walked through a park and a housing estate before finding a pub that contained several Portsmouth groups, the majority of which were worse for wear and annoying the locals in general. Apart from one group of about a dozen young local lads who were already on their first game of spoof and were oblivious to the rowdiness around them. Eventually we managed to summon a couple of cabs and got back to our hotel about 7.45 where we retrieved our bags from storage, had the quickest shower in historical record, and met up about 8.30 to sample the evening delights of Yeovil.

By now Jim was already at his limit of imperial alcoholic measure and I expected him to meet us in the lobby in his PJs; it was a surprise therefore that he'd donned his cords and was seemingly up for an evening's entertainment. Our room at the back of the hotel overlooked the local Wetherspoons offering and we decided that this would be our first stop. As a group we walked in to what was the emptiest Wetherspoons I'd ever known, and as a group we promptly walked straight out again. The reason being that apart from Yates' Wine Lodge in Leicester Square, I've never walked into a pub that smelt so badly of vomit. Even with a strong stomach I couldn't countenance the idea of staying there. When we walked back to our hotel later the place was heaving but I could only put this down to Yeovil women wearing overbearing amounts of perfume.

Strolling through the town centre we expected to find an alternative option pretty quickly but it was some 15 minutes before we stumbled upon The Mermaid. There was barely breathing space inside as I lined up at the bar next to a bloke with the most voluminous tattoos and piercings I'd ever seen. There was barely any part of him which had been naturally left exposed to the elements. I could imagine the caption on those late night comedy shows, what would be the least likely thing said by this person? The words "I'm comfortable in my own skin" sprang to mind – how I hate that pretentious phrase. Having eventually bought a round of drinks we went out to their beer garden (loosely described) where we froze for about half an hour before moving on to The Butcers Arms. OK it was actually The Butchers Arms but the H had dropped off the sign.

This was a proper locals pub. There were a couple of decent real ales on the pump, and bearing in mind that the girls had now moved on to jugs of tap water, Chop was restricted to half a wheat free cider and Steve's manflu had by now seen him off, it was a cheap round. Andy was flagging, which left Jim who was by now on about his seventh beer with no sign of wincyette in sight. As I paid for the round, I was tempted to mention to the landlord that his pub sign had dropped its' aitch, but he was an imposing figure and my impression was that he'd just reply that if I didn't like it I could sling my hook. Silence got the better of me. Which I wished it had got earlier before I opened my mouth in the taxi because I was repeatedly subjected to abuse about my Pompey Slappers aberration. It continued even after we were walking back to the hotel with Toni in particular dishing out a sly Beckhamesque kick to my shins as we walked behind them. Not being Latin American I resisted the temptation to collapse and roll around though I did brandish a yellow card.

The evening ended back at the Beefeater. We'd again passed on the Wetherspoons on the way back – I can't remember its actual name but it was something like The Sir Archibald Vomit and by now it was suddenly packed. Andy, me and surprisingly Jim – gagging for another pint – were the last men standing.

The following morning I blotted my copybook, this time with Michelle, when I tried to get my money back under the Premier Inn promise of money back if you don't get a good night's sleep. When asked why I hadn't slept well I replied that it was because my wife was snoring all night but I was advised this was not sufficient cause for a refund. I hadn't read the small print but felt it was a bit like the episode of The Simpsons where Homer had consulted his lawyer having been chucked out of the All You Can Eat buffet for eating too much.

Jim emerged to meet us after breakfast to have his – a quick roll up – and we chatted outside about our weekend away, specifically deciding upon suitable slogans a la Folke Golf Centre.

We plumped for the following:-

"Huish Park – where football is supposed to be entertaining."

"Radio taxis – where cabs are supposed to be plentiful"

"Yeovil – where pubs are supposed to smell good".

A couple of hours later, after successfully dodging the badger carcasses on the A303, we got to Fareham in time for Jim to sleep off the excesses of the night before and with time to spare before he emerged to play darts at 6.58 precisely and as usual..

Yeovil had been fun. I particularly enjoyed their friendly approach and excellent hospitality facilities.

Next stop Barnet, 3 days later

CHAPTER 14

BARNET

So I went to Barnet. We lost. It was crap. There's not much more to say, but for anyone ever thinking of going to Barnet, I will.

The Barnet game had originally been scheduled for the end of January, but due to our appearance in round 4 of the FA Cup it had been rescheduled. This had mortified Chop who had not only bought tickets for the game but also an overnight hotel nearby so he and Toni could have a night out in North London. He couldn't work out whether to flog his hotel room at a knock-down price on Gumtree or to scoot off from the Bournemouth cup game at Fratton and make his way up to London to get his moneys worth.

I was away for the original date so hadn't got a ticket, but he had a spare for the revised date. He was going to be up in London that day with work so I bought a £15 return to Waterloo on a winter promotion and arranged to meet up with him there.

I looked at Barnet on the tube map and then looked at where the ground was. They are in fact about 6 miles apart. Checking on Wikipedia, I found they had moved to The Hive in Edgware in 2013. The nearest stop to the ground was at Cannons Green which was virtually the entire length of the Jubilee Line away from Waterloo.

Barnet were the ultimate yoyo team. A bit like Burnley and West Brom between the Championship and Premiership, Barnet had been in and out of League and non-league. They had however for a lower league club nursed quite a few players on to Premier League teams, including Dougie Freedman, Jason "he poos when he wants" Puncheon, Yannick Bolasie, Marlon King (as in "she said no, Marlon, she said no") and our very own Linvoy Primus.

I looked at the Away Grounds Guide and realised that there were not going to be many places close to the ground where Chop and I could meet up. We decided on Moranos, a wine bar close to the tube station. Chop had got there quite early and was apparently nursing his solitary one-pint cider allowance until I arrived. I'd played the usual telephone tag with Chop to finally establish this. In fact I had been alerted to his whereabouts by Toni who'd sent me a text:-

"Chop has sent you a message. If you have a problem contacting him please contact me your local Pompey slapper as a go-between"

She doesn't forget easily, that one.

I found Moranos purely by pricking my ears and following the noise as I left the station. It wasn't really a pub, more a converted shopfront, and there was a queue outside. Chop told me that he'd got me a beer in, but it looked like I might struggle to get to drink it. There were a couple of bouncers on the door, supported by local police and it was one in one out. Finally getting to the front of the queue, I took a step forward to enter but was then told that the police had told them to stop anyone else going in however empty it might have become. Despite claiming my pint was waiting for me, they weren't budging. I started to trudge away, thirsty and disconsolate, and texted Chop to say that I'd meet him outside the tube station. I then got a text telling me to come back; it appeared Chop had charmed the landlady and I strolled back to be allowed entry.

I could see why the police had wanted the place to empty. It was loud and full. Half an hour before kick off at any Pompey away game there will always be a lively atmosphere but this was something else. I got the impression that a lot of the occupants had been there for some time. A lot were pretty stone drunk and the language and songs floating around the place were a bit more colourful than usual. I finished my beer quickly and went off in search of food.

There was a kebab shop nearby with a lengthy queue and I decided I'd chance my arm on the pies at the ground instead. To get to The Hive you walk through a park and on the way we got chatting to a Barnet fan, who, amongst other things, told me, I felt with some smugness, that they don't sell pies inside the ground at Barnet. I almost felt impertinent for suggesting that they should.

We reached the ground about 15 minutes before the game and the beer sales at the two food and drink kiosks were obviously swelling the Barnet coffers. I just wanted something hot, even if it was a cardboard burger. Finally getting to the front of the queue as the whistle blew for kick off, I was told that I was at the wrong kiosk for hot food. I asked somewhat irritated why the board on the kiosk advertised burgers and got the sort of reply that David Cameron gives at question time. Yet again disappointed I stuffed a cheese and tomato roll into my pocket and we walked round to sample the delights of the game.

The away terrace at The Hive is just like something out of the 1970s. a few barriers, not very deep, quite close to the pitch. We managed to find a spot to the right of the goal. At the other end was a covered stand which on this particular evening couldn't have contained more than a couple of hundred home supporters. There didn't really appear to be much if anything to our left, except the makeshift dug-outs. The stand to our right was the largest and seemingly the most modern, seating away supporters nearer our end and home supporters the other. In fact this game was unusual in that stats showed there were more away fans than home fans in the ground

We started with a familiar 4-2-3-1 formation. This never seemed to vary in form, only in substance, with the personnel in the most forward positions changing sometimes from game to game. Gareth Evans had not recovered from his knock on the previous Saturday and Adam McGurk had come in to replace him, with McNulty taking Michael Smith's spot leading the line. I hadn't seen a lot in Michael Smith to particularly impress me, although he worked hard, but equally, though I felt Mark McNulty was an excellent acquisition, always likely to score, I didn't see him as a lone striker. The general feeling amongst our group of fans was that although Cook obviously liked this formation, we'd never had the man up front to hold the ball up, win challenges in the air and run the channels, until Caolan Lavery, and now he had gone back to his parent club.

I wasn't wholly convinced by Adam McGurk either; he ran around a lot, won his fair share of ball in the air as well, but I couldn't shake off the feeling that he wasn't keen on the more physical side of the game. Against Barnet, managed by Mad Dog Martin Allen, that wasn't an option. From the start of this game we were physically inferior, through fair means or foul, and there was a lot of the latter. Gary Roberts was crunched early on and was replaced within 10 minutes by Kal Naismith, another who'd failed to really show that he was star quality. The first half passed in a blur, with no real chances either way, until just before half-time when Adam Webster gave away what appeared to be a rather softly awarded penalty, converted by ex-Pompey failure John Akinde, a typical lumbering physical League Two centre forward.

The highlight of the first half for the travelling support were the chants directed at the Head Steward who was wearing what everyone justifiably believed was a hairpiece. Credit to him, he took the stick well and even proffered a smiley wave back.

Half-time came and we met up with a couple of people we hadn't seen for some games (that's what I like about away games, you often come across people who've moved away from the area to live and work). We had a collective moan about our performance so far. It had been poor to say the least; the natives on the terrace around me, perhaps fuelled by a gallon of beer in some instances, were disaffected.

Like at Yeovil on the previous Saturday we appeared to have more appetite for the game in the second half. I did wonder if managerial instructions were to try to get to half-time at 0-0 and then push on in the second half. It sometimes seemed that way.

In the home defence was Bondz N'gala. He'd turned out for us for a number of games the previous season. He wasn't the most comfortable on the ball – in fact he'd made Joe Devera look like Maradona – and he had an aversion to kicking any ball which might conceivably be headed instead. There was a reason for that; he was so poor on the deck that on one occasion the previous year against Wimbledon he'd sliced a clearance on the half way line and given away a corner. In our household he was nicknamed Spongebob Squareboots.

So it was no surprise what happened in the second half when a cross came in from the left about a foot off the ground. Realising that if he kicked the ball it would be 50:50 as to which direction it would fly , Bondz chose the headed option instead and somehow the ball got stuck under his prostrate body, with a few howls for handball. It was cringeworthy to watch and begged two questions. First, what was I doing in North West London on a Tuesday night when I could be in the pub watching Arsenal v Barcelona? Second, did we have any chance of promotion if we couldn't beat a team with this level of skill-set?

There was no lack of effort second-half and we were better but only had one real chance when Adam McGurk's header was pushed on to the bar by their 'keeper. Our night was summed up when Enda Stevens got in behind their defence only for his cross to elude all of our (well 2) onrushing strikers and ending up as a Barnet throw half way down the pitch. There was just time for Conor Chaplin to be given his statutory 8 minutes game-time. I'd come to the conclusion that someone had bought Paul Cook a Conor Chaplin egg-timer for Christmas, one where the sand passed through after 82 minutes of normal time. It certainly seemed that way, and on this occasion it was insufficient for him to make an impact as the game fizzled out into another away defeat.

But not before the natives got very restless indeed. I don't think I could remember such vitriol being hurled at our own players at an away game. The defeat would put us out of not only the automatic promotion spots but also the play-off places. Frustration, at what had started as a season when we looked nailed on for promotion, really came to the fore this night in north London, and it wasn't pretty.

Over in the corner of the ground, the atmosphere became even more rancid as police started scanning the away terrace with miniature hand-held video cameras. I don't know why they thought this might be helpful, but it just seemed provocative. Most of the crowd were just accepting of yet another disappointing performance, it was the few rather than the many who were becoming agitated. Yet even I felt a little resentful about being scanned by a video camera like a prisoner in an exercise yard. Others quite clearly were more irate about this intrusion; one bloke ended up face to face with one policeman who was videoing him at close range, taking a video back on his 'phone, like High Noon with cameras. It all seemed to me something of an ill-judged police exercise.

Mercifully, the final whistle blew. Some players walked

over to the away end but there was little if any applause. Most fans like me just wanted to trudge away into the night, no boos but no plaudits either. Skipper Michael Doyle clearly felt an "apology" was in order for the performance. He was met by a lot of abuse. As a Pompey fan I was disappointed by that. He wasn't one who could ever be accused of not giving all, or shirking a tackle, but like pretty much everyone in a blue shirt, he'd had a bit of a shocker. That for me doesn't justify abuse of that magnitude, and I felt sorry for him. We aren't talking about guys on 50k a week here. I doubt if a lot of our players now earn six figures a year in a career which is short. So in my book it was OK to boo Jermaine Defoe when he didn't move his expensive backside off the same blade of grass when he was itching for a move back from Pompey to his beloved Spurs; but not to players who'd tried but failed, as was the case at Barnet.

In the car as we sped past Wembley on the circular, Chop and I debated where we went from here. Fortunately, I knew where I was going – a fortnight in Cambodia to meet up with Paddy on his travels. I was almost relieved, having seen two poor games in four days, to have a break from it.

When I got home, I realised that it was almost a year to the day since Dagenham the previous season. I told Michelle that when we got our 2017 calendar we were to cross through February with the words NO MIDWEEK AWAY GAMES IN LONDON.

CHAPTER 15

MANSFIELD

I have nothing but good memories of my Junior School days living in Hilsea.on the north of Portsea island. Endless days playing football at Alexandra Park. Being allowed to stay up to watch Match of the Day to watch my favourite players George Best and Bobby Charlton. Getting a Manchester United shirt for Christmas or some George Best Stylo Matchmakers for my birthday. But so many things were different to the present day. For a start, all the local kids supported Pompey first. The Liverpool and Man United shirts were for their second favourite teams. If Pompey dabbled in replica shirts in the 1960s, we'd have got them for Christmas instead.

Footballs were not coated. They had a bladder inside which was blown up after each game, and we took turns in the school football team to take the ball home to dubbin it for the next game. You really didn't want to head that ball on the lace on a wet day. I'm sure that there would be a Health and Safety report upon the dangers of heading a ball like that if they were still being used today. And what about the school football socks which had the foot cut out, with an elastic gusset that you wore over your own pair of football socks, with shin pads about an inch thick. I look back at my Junior school football team photo and marvel at how anyone could manoeuvre with lower legs covered with all this kit. It looks a bit like Michael Phelps wearing a woolly jumper for the Olympic freestyle final or Chris Hoy wearing jeans with bicycle clips. Health and Safety was an unknown concept. I recall playing one Saturday morning game against Flying Bull Lane school when I flew into a tackle at Alex Park on an icy morning and cut my wrist open. It would probably these days be front page news in the local rag but all that happened was that our teacher/manager Mr. Smith wrapped a handkerchief around the wound to stop the blood flow and said "get back on there son".

My Dad's parents always called in after their weekly trip to Charlotte Street to buy their vegetables for the week. My grandad would always ask how we'd got on that morning and when I told him of another handsome victory (my Junior school cuttings show that we won 14 out of 14 that year) his response would always be the same – "who were you playing – the Blind School?" Sensitivities regarding disabilities were not high on the agenda in the 1960s.

I remember the Esso promotions. I got my Dad to fill up his Ford Consul a gallon at a time to have more chance of completing my 1970 England World Cup coin collection (unsuccessfully as it happened) or the complete collection of Esso football club badges which are still up in the loft, though getting Man City proved to be so elusive that I eventually only completed the collection by giving up my entire swap collection to a kid who no doubt went on to become a skilled hostage negotiator.

My favourite school day was Tuesday. Firstly because the Corona man always came round to deliver Ice Cream Soda on a Tuesday night and secondly because I went to bed knowing that Shoot! Magazine would be on the doormat the following day.

It was Shoot! magazine which gave me my unjustifiably romantic notion of Mansfield. At the start of every season,

Shoot! magazine gave out a free gift of a cardboard cut out league table for all 4 divisions. The cardboard tabs for each team were in their club colours. You would press them out and spend Saturday evening making up the revised league tables by reference to the Football Mail.

Most teams were red or blue and their tabs were pretty boring but the Mansfield tab was a flamboyant orange and black. At the time they were in the old Division 4 and I looked out for their results after ours every week. I decided that one day I'd visit Mansfield for a game as an honorary supporter, wherever it was. It became my own personal Brigadoon.

So it was, some 45 years later that I was going to get my wish. I had asked Andy to get the tickets while I was on holiday, and just the two of us were making the trip. While I'd been away, we'd suddenly found our form, winning against Cambridge at home and following up with a draw at Exeter (and it could have been better, leading until the last minute before yet another last minute equaliser reduced a 3 point haul to one) However we'd won away at Stevenage and then picked up a big three points in the re-arranged game at Accrington in what sounded our best performance of the season. On my last night in Cambodia I had gone to bed at ten to catch an early bus back to Phnom Penh the following morning. Being 7 hours ahead I couldn't risk sleeping through the alarm the following morning but I hit the sack confident that I'd wake up to another 3 points in the bag at home to Newport. Barnet was forgotten, I was itching to get back to the fray.

I woke about 5 the next morning and flicked on my iPad for the result. In typical Pompey fashion it was a 3-0 defeat with reports of about 10 fans being left in the ground come the final whistle. Dan, who'd used my ticket for the match, sent me a message saying it had been the worst he'd seen all season. Suddenly the trip to Mansfield was looking less enticing.

I arranged to pick Andy up about 8.30, aiming on 4 hours

to Mansfield. The journey was smooth apart from Saturday morning shoppers going into Birmingham, and even with the usual stop at Warwick services – I wonder how much cash they've relieved me of in the past year – we were twenty minutes away by midday. Yet again Andy's bladder dictated another stop, but half an hour later, we parked up in our hotel called "281" rooms, which was on the main road into Mansfield and only a mile from the ground and the town centre.

Leaving the bags in the car, we decided to check out the action, which did not include comparing the price of the broccoli in the Sainsburys superstore or strolling in to one of the many fitness centres that we passed on the way to the town. With that many gyms I expected half the blokes we met to be ripped and ready to take on Tyson Fury, but in fact Mansfield seemed a pretty normal place and quite a trim little town. Certainly, the houses we passed were neat and tidy, the type of 1930s detached and semi-detached character properties which cost about half a million just off Portsea Island, but which the estate agents windows suggested could be bought at less than half that amount in Mansfield. With three top-100 golf courses nearby, I ventured that it would be a good place to trade down, and decided to mention this to Michelle when I got home, though omitting to mention the golf courses.

One of the houses we passed had a very neat front garden, even in mid–March the lawn looked like it had been cut with scissors, and the flower beds were immaculate, except that they weren't flower beds, but vegetable beds each laid out with carefully marked wooden stakes identifying what was planted where. Neat as it was, it looked like an invitation to a late night Saturday reveller to nab some free veg for Sunday dinner. "What veg do you want with the roast beef tomorrow, sweetheart? Carrots and parsnips? Righto, I'll just hop over the wall at number 199 on the way back from the pub later".

Passing a fellow on the corner of one road he offered a friendly good afternoon and we exchanged pleasantries. As we strolled on, Andy suggested that wouldn't happen in North End. Well, they might say "All right mush?" but they'd punch you first as a precaution.

We passed the Talbot Arms which was for home fans only, and decided to give Il Rosso, on the opposite side of the road, a miss. Even though it apparently showed live football it looked a bit posh for us. Carrying on to the town we came upon The Railway Inn which held a mix of home, away and completely disinterested punters. We couldn't find a seat and although their array of real ales was interesting and the steak and kidney pudding looked enticing, we moved on to the main square.

There was a host of options in Mansfield Town centre; though some had closed and were apparently looking for new landlords to be suckered in to paying the high rents that most breweries seem to charge. It reminded me a little of Beverley where I'd stayed a few years back while taking in a Hull away game. Beverley was one of my favourite places, nice housing, a great Saturday farmers market and a huge selection of good pubs in the market square. Mansfield was not in the same class as Beverley but as an away day venue it far outshone the out of town stadiums I'd visited which had little if any nearby infrastructure.

We settled on the Wetherspoons called The Courthouse, which suited me because it was my round and I got a pound change from a fiver for a couple of beers. Andy chatted for a while to a guy who sits near him at home games, and we tried without success to blag a plate of scampi for which, in the vast expanses of the pub, the waitress was struggling to find a home. My Mum and her mate love their two for one Monday steaks at 'Spoons and I've taken advantage of their full English a couple of times after a heavier night. But I've not been tempted much to eat there after Paddy came home one day saying that he'd not been able to get a couple of poached eggs on toast because they'd run out of boil in the bag poached eggs. I can understand the need for mass catering to keep the prices at the sort of level they charge, but I'd rather pay 50p more and have my egg poached in a pan.

We went in search of a big screen to catch the second half of the lunchtime game, and crossed the square with its' lively Saturday market. There were lots of options, unlike Yeovil, and we eventually decided on The Swan on the corner of Church Street. We'd barely got our drinks when in walked a couple of familiar faces from school, Mark Parnell (Parny) and Andy Vernon (AV). Strangely, I'd actually seen Parny at Barnet but hadn't seen AV for years. I'd read though with some surprise that for a while he'd been chairman at Petersfield Town and he told us how he'd ended up there after managing Moneyfields Wessex League reserve side, which was made up of a number of players who were released by Pompey as kids.

Parny showed us on his 'phone a photo of an old school football team and we tried to work out which year it was taken. The fact that Billy Clark was wearing a jumbo collar shirt under his football shirt suggested 1973. We got chatting about our old first eleven, where Parny played midfield and AV was a regular sub even though he was two years younger. Ken Hoad was a geography teacher who also ran the First Eleven. I'd not seen or heard of him for many years until I was invited to the local referee's association golf day, where I noticed Ken's name on the list, though I guessed he would now be in his late 70s. AV then mentioned he'd come across him while playing local league football in his mid-20s. Ken was refereeing one game where AV had taken out a forward pretty badly. He said the subsequent conversation went as follows:-

"Andrew, up you get and come here." AV walks over for the lecture.

KEN: Andrew, what's the capital of Portugal?

AV: Lisbon?

KEN: Good lad, I'm glad you learned something. But you're still going in the book.

I don't know if that's true but Andy Vernon always told a good yarn.

Time had moved on and we were now in danger of missing kick-off, having reminisced like only 50-something blokes can do. So we made our way towards the ground, with Parny getting on his phone and using his Googlemaps to take us in entirely the wrong direction, even though he insisted he'd been to Mansfield before. Perceptively Andy and I suggested that the ground might possibly be in the opposite direction where we could see the floodlights, and, Parny begrudgingly making a detour from his 'phone directions we got to Field Mill, Mansfield's ground, right on kick-off.

It was a familiar 4-2-3-1 line up, with Michael Smith again up front on his own and behind him McNulty, Bennett and Naismith, who'd been brought in for the injured Gary Roberts. We parked ourselves in seats near the front and yawned as the first 15 minutes passed with barely a chance for either side.

The uneventful nature of the game allowed us to look around the stadium. Not unusually in League Two the largest and most impressive stand ran the length of the pitch. The away fans were located in a smaller but covered stand and the home end was a modest affair, sparsely populated. The majority were in the stand running the length of the pitch. To some extent this is where most football grounds have changed since the 1970s terraced structures. In those days The Stretford end, the Kop, The North Bank and The Shed end were all known as exclusively for the hard core home support. In most Ikea flat pack grounds these days, even the most passionate, it's hard to know where the most ardent supporters actually sit. It's the same in League Two. I can't remember one game when I could recognise one of the ends behind the goal as housing the hardcore fans, maybe with the exception of Bristol Rovers.

Like a few other grounds, Mansfield was also missing a fourth stand. The whole of the area to my left looked like the Berlin Wall post 1990, populated only by the home and away dugouts.

The game was quite dull, and suddenly feeling the hunger resulting from our overstaying our welcome in The Swan, I took advantage of an injury break to buy Chicken Tikka pies, which hit the spot nicely on what was an increasingly chilly afternoon. And soon after the pies hit the spot, the referee pointed to the spot as Mark McNulty was brought down making his way to the by-line. It looked a bit soft, but not as soft as the same player's penalty which was saved well by the Mansfield 'keeper to collective groans in the away end.

Just before the penalty, I'd had a chat with Paul Taylor, who had worked with the buy-out team on the administration in preparing the first three years budgets. He had set off with about 10 mates at about 6.30 in the morning, travelling up to Mansfield in a party limo. They were a pretty noticeable party as they were all in Blues Brothers kit. The You Tube highlights the following day showed Paul behind the goal when the penalty was saved, putting his head in his hands. But in fairness it could probably have been everyone else in the 1000 plus contingent from the South Coast. Missing penalties is just so Pompey. Apart from when we had Kevin Dillon in the 70s and 80s and Alan McLoughlin in the 80s and 90s. They never missed.

Within 10 minutes we were one down. A route one goal where we missed the first header and their striker latched on to the flick-on. Our on loan 'keeper Ryan Fulton obviously had a thing about not being beaten at his near post but on this occasion it meant that their striker had the whole of the far side of the goal to aim at and he planted it beyond a despairing dive into the centre of the goal.

We covered our heads in despair and I saw Paul Taylor disappear for another bladder discharge. We looked so poor. But just before half time we won a corner and Ben Davies' kick was met at the far post by their right back's left bollock. Unfortunately for him the bollock was facing his own goal and we somehow had equalised. Ben gave a celebration of sorts but the rest of our team trotted back sheepishly to the half way line. Own goals had just become our top scorers for the month.

We somehow believed that Mansfield would be like Yeovil and that we would come out invigorated for the second half. It just never happened though. Despite Paul Cook looking like he was having a thrombie in the dug out, the second half passed without virtually any form of incident.

We were glad to hear the final whistle, bade our farewells to Parny and AV and started our walk back to the hotel. On the way we stopped off at Sainsburys, not to check whether the broccoli was on offer but so that Andy could empty his overworked bladder and I bought a couple of coffees to warm us through.

Back at the hotel, I gained a realisation that Portsmouth must be a good visit for the tourism industry of the average League two town. I hadn't noticed this before but there must have been four different couples or groups in Pompey shirts chewing the fat over what they had just watched. I doubt if the Portsmouth tourist industry made a lot of money when Mansfield came to town but I reckon that half their "281" rooms were taken up by Portsmouth fans staying overnight. I wondered how much away football fans were worth to smaller Premier League clubs. For example, how many Geordies and Mackems make a weekend out of a 320 mile trip to Southampton? If things carried on like they were panning out, the Reading hotel trade might be coining it in if Newcastle and Sunderland were relegated. Whatever division they are in, they always have a huge away following.

We went straight up to our room, checked our ipads and realised we'd even now slipped out of the play-off places. We mulled over our form and our formation. It was ironic to both of us that while in the previous year Andy Awford had persisted with wing backs when we really didn't have the players for that formation, this year we seemed to have the perfect set of players for 3-5-2 and yet we continued playing a flat back four, two holding midfield players and only one up front. Instead we could play three solid centre halves, a couple of offensive full-backs and have the potential for two forwards as opposed to a lone striker who didn't convince in the role.

Contemplating the evening ahead. I had a quick shower and couldn't resist a nap; it's an age thing. I hoped that Andy wasn't going to suggest that we hit the town square again. Fortunately, he was happy with the suggestion that we stroll down the road, have a couple of pints and a bit of grub and take in the last game of the Six Nations.

It was a toss-up between the Italian wine bar and The Talbot Arms. The latter got the vote for two reasons. First because they still had a blackboard outside the pub saying "Home fans only" and we were feeling like James Dean in Rebel Without a Cause. Second because the equivalent grub in the Italian wine bar was about a fiver more expensive. We found a table, had a couple of beers and a passable chicken with chorizo and settled in to watch England playing for the Grand Slam in Paris.

I never played rugby – or for that matter cricket – at school, but as I aged I was beginning to appreciate both. Rugby Union had a lot to commend it. No cheating or diving, replacements leaving and entering the field of play in a run, and the excellent application of the advantage rule. I considered how many football players would try to ride a foul tackle in the penalty area if they thought they might achieve some personal glory by staying on their feet confident in the knowledge that if they didn't score personally, they might have a penalty to fall back on. I used to quite like Jamie Redknapp as a football pundit until the day he commented on a player taking a blatant dive by saying "He was entitled to go down". No, he wasn't and that comment epitomised everything wrong about modern day football and the cheating which was endemic within it.

But much as I had come to enjoy watching rugby, I still couldn't give it any credit for one thing; the scoring system seemed to me to be all to cock. On the evening we watched England play France, the English played flowing rugby and were the better side by a country mile. Yet half way through the second half, there were very few points between the teams because the French had scored a bundle of penalties. I just don't get this. You can be 10 yards from the opposing line and the opposition commit an offence. You kick a penalty and it's three points. Equally, you can barely escape your own half, the opposition commit an offence and it's the same 3 points. How can this be right? Surely, if you are only just in the opposition's half there should be some risk and reward; you can kick for goal for one point or you can kick for touch and go for a much more lucrative 5. Being able to score a significant number of points from a long range penalty is a bit like someone in football tugging an opponent's shirt on the half way line and then conceding a free kick at goal from that spot with all of the opposition players being told to leave the pitch while the penalty taker has a free shot.

I've raised this point with Rugby aficionados in my office and they say it's all because rugby is a game based on discipline. But I think it's more that it's a case of "that's the way we've always allocated points" and they're just happy to continue that way. Sorry, but I still don't get why it's fair that one team can be so much superior to another but can still lose because the opposition has one bloke out of 15 who can kick the ball long and straight.

As it happened, England did win the Grand Slam anyway, but by the time the game had finished we were ready to get back to our hotel to watch the end of Match of the Day. There were still a few Pompey fans in the 281 rooms as we had a Gin and Tonic to finish off the night. There was also a birthday bash going on in the function room but we weren't tempted to try to gatecrash. Instead we nodded off in front of the TV with our bedtime G and Ts and a bag of Liquorice Allsorts which I'd salvaged from the car.

We made a fairly early start the following morning, heartened by a cooked breakfast with a proper sausage as opposed to mass-produced gristle. The sun was shining and spring was in the air, at least until we got about 5 miles down the road. Our journey home was uneventful until just north of Oxford on the A34, when I spotted a police van with flashing lights steaming down the outside lane of the dual carriageway. I promptly pulled into the inside lane as did cars in front of and behind me. But as the van passed us it was apparent that he wanted to be off at the next slip road. I couldn't see what the car in front of us could do as the slip road loomed close, other than slam on his anchors and probably cause an accident. As it happened the police van swerved across the chevrons onto the slip road. But the unbelievable thing that followed was that an arm came out of the driver's side window of the van. As we passed by Andy said to me "Did I just see what I thought I saw?" I replied "Yep, the copper driving the van gave the driver in the car the finger."

Well, see Chapter 8. We are talking about Oxford police. Why was I not surprised.

CHAPTER 16

YORK

Every year in the early spring I have a meet-up with my old flatmates from Newcastle Poly. There were three of them and because we were all around the country, the weekend would always be in London. Chis was an armchair Man United fan who had stayed in Newcastle after his degree and was now a teacher at a school which took in those kids who'd been expelled from all the others. Pat had lived in Ripon, moved down to Trowbridge for a while and was now living in Harrogate and working in York in the Health Service. Dave also lived in Ripon when he was at Poly, but because of family connections supported Norwich. He'd moved around in the MOD to Cambridge and then Bristol where he'd finally taken early retirement.

Our annual routine was fairly established by now. Late afternoon arrival, a few beers and a bit of grub on the Friday, a museum tour or maybe a tour of Lords or Wimbledon on the Saturday morning, in the bookies for a bet on the football and taking in a match on the Saturday afternoon. Every year we'd gone to Craven Cottage because it is and was one of the few places in the top division where it was possible to get tickets as a neutral, and, well, because it's just a proper football ground. This year it was going to be on the weekend we were at home to Wycombe, another home match that I'd miss.

After Mansfield, it had been tempting to throw in the towel and abandon my away fest for the year. But we then had three wins on the bounce, at home to Notts County and Carlisle and away at Dagenham, who were by now doomed to relegation. We were firmly back in the play off places, and with a six-pointer coming up at home to Plymouth, I looked again at the possibilities for a final away game before the end of the season. There were only three options, and one wasn't an option because yet again I hadn't managed to get a ticket for the over-subscribed game at Wimbledon. The old Plough Lane had been one of my regular visits back in the 70s and 80s but I'd never been successful in getting a ticket now that they only had room for about 500 away fans at Kingston. This is something which may surprise many people who have never taken much notice of lower league football; it can be as hard for a supporter of a club with a large away following, like ours, to get a ticket at say Wimbledon, Crawley, Dagenham or Barnet, as it is for an Arsenal fan to get a ticket at Bournemouth or Palace. It seemed odd to me that with revenue so low in League two it was not possible to come up with a solution whereby a bit of imagination was used to increase an away allocation of tickets when a ground is only going to be half-populated with home fans.

But moan or not, it wasn't going to happen at Wimbledon; and Hartlepool was out of the question because my brother-in-law Michael had arranged a surprise weekend in Dublin for Denise's 60th. Michelle wanted to go and I had to confess that a weekend in Dublin marginally had the edge over a weekend away in Hartlepool. I did ponder whether I should suggest to Michelle that we ask Mike whether we could house sit for them in Durham (which would leave me a short trip across to the Monkey-Hangers) but temerity and self-preservation got the better of me and the thought soon passed.

Which left York, which was on the Tuesday before my annual meet-up with the old Poly boys in London. I did think how odd it was that the fixtures computer had come up with such a long midweek trip. The same had happened on the reverse fixture which was also on a Tuesday. I had got pretty fed up in the Premier League when a long distance away game had been moved to 5.30 on a Saturday just to suit Sky or BT but I didn't expect that I'd have to travel from Kings landing to Winterfell – in Game of Thrones terms – for a midweek game in League Two.

I managed to change my days at work to take the Tuesday and Wednesday off to allow a trip up on the road on Tuesday, an overnighter and a journey back on the Wednesday. I also suggested to Andy that we could on the way back on the Wednesday take in a game of golf at Frilford Heath near Oxford which was a top 100 golf course and which was on the route home. Getting wind of this, Pete, who'd not seen a Pompey game since Cheltenham the previous season, expressed an interest, so I provisionally booked a triple room in a pub on the outskirts of York, at Fulford, and rang Pat to see what he might be able to sort out in the way of hospitality.

While at Poly, Pat had been a Leeds fan when they were in the old Division One. He'd actually played a few games for York Reserves before he came to Newcastle, and he maintained that his claim to fame or notoriety was that he'd accidentally broken Cec Podd's leg in a reserve game against Bradford. Cec Podd was one of the few black players around in the 70s but Pat insisted there was nothing racist in the challenge.

Since he'd taken up his job in York, he'd once again formed a bond with the football club. In truth he had become disillusioned with top flight football and had come to appreciate the wholehearted no-nonsense honesty of lower division football. It was a bit like the Wolf of Wall Street turning Socialist. However, the fact was that he was now on the road to Damascus to the extent that he had become a Vice-President at York City. In lower league terms I don't think this meant much more than him putting in an enhanced sum each year for the right to pre-match hospitality for himself and his guests and to take a seat in the Director's box. He e-mailed me back quickly to say that for the princely sum of £30 each we could join him in the Vice-President's lounge for some modest match hospitality, and a seat each in the Director's box behind the Portsmouth Directors. It was too good to pass up, especially as the alternative was to stand on the exposed away terrace.

On the Saturday beforehand, we had a home 6-pointer against Plymouth. They were on a bit of a dodgy run and we'd won three on the bounce. If we won, an automatic promotion spot was pretty much within our own destiny and we would not have to rely on others to slip up.

As expected, Fratton Park was full for this game and the Plymouth fans took their allocation as well, so the atmosphere was lively. We dominated the game and took a lead in the first half, but as had become the story of our season, we failed to convert chances to put the game beyond reach. Plymouth had been a shadow of the team I'd seen on highlights for much of the season, but within the last ten minutes we gifted them two pretty sloppy goals, one from a cross where Paul Jones had been outjumped by their centre forward Jamille Matt, the second as a result of allowing them far too much space down the right and standing off them in the 6 yard box. Once again we trudged home wondering how we had lost to a team who had been wholly inferior for so much of the game.

Suddenly a long trip to York was not looking quite so enticing. We now needed to pretty much win every game to have a chance of an automatic spot. But at least our next game was against a team who, like Dagenham, who we had thrashed a couple of weeks beforehand, were all but relegated, and who were shipping goals at the same rate that Fyffes ship bananas into Pompey.

So it was that on Tuesday 19th April, we hooked up about 11 and after sailing around the M25, we hit the M1 and made our way up to York. Sarah the satnav brought me in to York on a fairly circuitous route but I think it was because she wanted me to enjoy the Area of Outstanding Natural Beauty that is the power station between Ferrybridge and Selby. Sight seeing accomplished without stopping, we got to our pub hotel about 4.15. I parked up the car tight to the wall, keen to ensure that no-one could access our boot to appropriate my 15 year old Ping irons from their final resting place. In so doing I gently pranged the car against the wall not once but twice, much to the mirth of the others – and believe me, having Andy take the piss out of your driving skills is the ultimate humiliation.

A quick check-in to a fairly spartan but clean room and we dived downstairs for a beer in the front garden. It was a lovely day and along with others who obviously didn't do much work either, we basked in short sleeves. Our hotel was about 3 miles outside the city centre and on the main bus route so we paid the 70p rather than order a taxi. This is something which would be totally alien to any of my kids. "A bus? What, really, you're suggesting I get a bus?" Admittedly, they aren't as frequent as when I was a kid, but still…

Steve and Sue had enjoyed a long weekend in York and we'd arranged to meet him in the Three-Legged Mare which was near the Minster in High Petergate and not too far to walk to the ground. We walked through York City Centre which was delightful, with its quaint pedestrian streets and upmarket shops. I couldn't resist a slight detour to walk into The Shambles which I remembered from 30 years or so earlier when I'd last visited Pat and his wife Gail, when touring the country cheaply in a beaten-up Morris Marina.

Steve and Sue were already in situ when we found the Three Legged Mare about 5.30. Sue was reading a Times in the corner, and was bemoaning the fact that York's museums shut down at 4pm. Steve on the contrary looked quite content with this restricted opening time as he smirked with what may have been his third pint of ale nestled on the table. There was a decent range of ale on the hand pull, the pub wasn't packed and we were soon joined by Pat and another local guest he was taking to the game. At one stage I strolled into the back garden and found a pocket of the Pompey Northern supporters being pictured with their flag. In fact I think they may have even come down from Scotland. They seemed almost distraught that we might get promoted and their short trips to Carlisle, York, Morecambe and Hartlepool might be lost never to return.

We were later joined by Duncan, Steve's brother, and Mick, who had spent the weekend before at some sort of dodgy festival in Sheffield. They were in turn joined by a mate of Mick's proudly wearing his York shirt. We got into one of those discussions where we were trying to outdo each other as to which of our supported teams had given us most grief this season. It was much different than you'd find if the discussion was between Arsenal and Chelsea. Such is the humility in League Two . Well, maybe not always, if you've seen the You Tube "you want some, I'll give you some" clip of the Wealdstone Raider telling opposing fans that their support was "shit".

It was time to leave for our hospitality. Pat had been trying to dampen expectations of a culinary masterpiece, but we were anxious to sample the salt beef rolls and roast potatoes which would constitute our pre-match grub. Bootham Crescent is just on the edge of the town centre, and we walked there in about 20 minutes past a row of 4 storey student houses that looked like they probably guaranteed an income of about £3000 a month for their landlord.

We ordered and paid for our drinks in the Vice-President's Lounge and read our complimentary programmes. It was Pat's turn to write the Vice-President's column and he encouraged me to read it, but the team sheets then arrived and I became distracted when checking whether we were playing our tried and trusted 4-2-3-1 formation once again.

It was then that we noticed Gareth Southgate on the next table, and imposed ourselves upon him, probably much to his despair. We did manage to establish that in his role with the England set-up, he was there to have a look at our defender Adam Webster and York's young striker Bradley Fewster. In fairness, he was amiable and talked freely to the extent that none of us even began to think of mentioning "that" missed penalty

It was time to take our seats, and we were directly behind the Directors, my seat being the one behind Mark Catlin our CEO. It would nonetheless be some overstatement to describe the Director's Box as plush.

Though this was a game we had to win, you wouldn't have thought so. We looked sluggish from the outset. In just the first minute they chased us down and a shot deflected about 45 degrees off Adam Webster's backside for a corner. The referee, just yards away, inexplicably signalled a goal kick and a bloke sitting in the seats adjacent to the Director's box let loose a tirade of abuse of such venom and at such volume that I half-expected a Local Authority Noise Inspector to turn up with a decibel device. He continued like this throughout the game, his face becoming redder and redder, and I seriously wondered if he would survive the ninety minutes. We laughed more and more as he got more and more uptight.

Gareth Southgate was to see more of Fewster than Webster because Adam had to come off with an injury mid-way through the first half. Had he stayed on the pitch this particular evening I don't think it would have made any difference. The already doomed York were playing with a freedom and hunger that we didn't match and by half-time we were two down, the first being a particularly poor goal to concede from a corner where not one but two free headers were allowed to the opposition. The second came from a slick move down the right with the cross being slotted home at the near post.

We trudged disconsolately down to the Lounge for half time tea and biscuits. Pat was euphoric and we could hardly begrudge him or York a two goal lead. We seemed to be suffering a hangover from those two late goals the previous Saturday. Our normally reliable holding pair of Hollands and Doyle were getting a bit of a runaround and striker Michael Smith had received little service. We just hoped that we'd repeat the Dagenham half-time comeback where we'd been 1-0 down at the break before winning 4-1.

It wasn't to be. Shortly after the break their midfielder Luke Summerfield was given acres of space to run at our defence and release a long range shot which Jones was never going to get near. Although we pulled a goal back after a goalkeeping error, we never looked like getting another and even our substitutions looked half-hearted.

But there was a moment in the second half which I thought summed up our style this season. Danny Hollands won a free-kick half way down the York half on the left side. Virtually every other team in the division would have taken stock, brought the guys up from the back, and launched the ball into the box hoping for a head to get on the ball or at least a knockdown. Instead, Danny put the ball down, passed it two yards to Michael Doyle and we ended up passing the ball across the back and eventually to our 'keeper who then launched the ball forward. I couldn't see the point of this and made this comment to Andy. Even our CEO turned round and seemed to be equally as curious, though in fairness to all of our representatives in the Director's box, none really gave away the slightest hint of being totally frustrated at what was a disastrous evening for us.

York ran out 3-1 winners and deserved it, but were effectively relegated that night. Like Cheltenham the season before I hoped they'd be back soon.

We chewed the fat for an hour in The Bootham Tavern, and then Pat took his leave. I was to see him the following weekend anyway, with a curry in Brick Lane, a tour of the Rolling Stones Exhibition, and Fulham v Forest all lined up.

With an early start the following morning to get to Oxford for golf, we jumped in a taxi where I managed to find myself in the front seat sharing conversation with a driver with a voice like a Dalek. A normal voice is a challenge to my deafnesss, but this one just left me nodding hopefully at every sentence.

Our chances of automatic promotion had effectively ended at York. It now looked like the play-offs.

I managed to sleep through Andy's hourly visits to the bathroom and we made our way down for an early breakfast. We were seemingly the only overnighters and the chef stayed around for a chat after he'd served up our full English. Like happens so often, the connection was the Navy. He had fond recollections of the Mighty Fine and the City Arms. We didn't like to tell him that the only locals who went near those places were skatebait.

Our journey home was clear apart from some roadworks just off the M1 at Towcester. When I say roadworks I mean cones because nobody seemed to be working. It added a good 20 minutes to our journey. I suggested to Andy, who was in the back seat, that we should slalom into the "works only" lane, and that he should put his hand out of the window tipping over all the cones as I zoomed away – but we resisted the temptation. At the end of the cones was a works van with MOBILE WELFARE UNIT written on the side. We guessed that this was why there was no workforce; they were all in there drinking tea. Alternatively, we thought that it might be a van for counselling the guys who were traumatised by their cones being deliberately knocked over.

After a stop off at Frilford Heath – well worth a visit although a bit stiff on the green fee – and handing over with great bitterness a fiver to Andy for his winnings, we got home early evening. It was only then that I fished out the programme to have a proper read of Pat's column in the programme, the first part of which is reproduced below:-

"May I extend a particularly warm welcome to the management, players and supporters of Portsmouth to Bootham Crescent this evening. The fixture computer clearly has had a field day by insisting that our visitors have had to endure one of the longest trips in our division on a Tuesday night, not the most convenient for supporters, but if you are an avid reader of the Vice-Presidents notes you may recall I have mentioned this before! Ridiculous and avoidable."

"What makes this evening extra special for me is that I will be joined by my close friend Chris who has been a Pompey fan all his life and has followed them over the years during the proverbial thick and (very) thin. Chris and I met when we were students in Newcastle in the late 70s when Portsmouth were languishing in the Fourth Division with an illustrious history well and truly behind them . Having been the first former League champions to be relegated into the third division in 1961 and after yo-yoing between the second and third divisions they finally sank to the bottom tier in 1978. The club has enjoyed what can only be described as an eventful history since then, peaking in most peoples' minds during Harry Redknapp's tenure by winning the FA Cup in 2008. Chris would have you believe that the visit of AC Milan, with the likes of Ronaldinho, Kaka and Shevechenko in their line up in the UEFA Cup was the true pinnacle, but only because he could then claim he himself had graced the very changing room that some of the greatest players in the world at that time had used. There is always one…"

Arsehole.

EPILOGUE

York was to be my last away game of the season. The records will show that we won three out of our last four games but the York defeat had been the last throw of the automatic promotion dice. Ending up sixth, we drew Plymouth in the play-offs and the timing of the games was not kind to me due to the annual boys golf week, this year in Majorca, straddling the two games. I watched the home leg in a bar in Palma, we were the better side but once again we had a soft underbelly in our own six-yard box and the game ended 2-2.

While I was on holiday, Nic tried to get us tickets for the away game but they sold out in just two hours. It was almost inevitable that we succumbed to an injury time goal, yet again bundled in from a corner from close range. My first thought was that I'd finally had it with Pompey, but the following day I reminded myself of the second half of Pat's programme notes which read as follows:-

"According to Wikipedia, what followed in subsequent years was "administration and three relegations, joining us in League Two in 2013 but, perhaps more importantly, they became the largest fan-owned club in April of that year. The likes of Chris and the many hundreds who have travelled north for the match tonight really are the lifeblood of this famous old club and they visit us this evening hoping to cement a play-off place. I wish them all the best over the coming weeks but not at our expense tonight"

"So why am I telling you this? Well – without a relative miracle we (the club, you and I) face relegation at the end of this campaign. Portsmouth have experienced highs that far exceed anything we have had and therefore their relative failure must be much harder to take. At a time when the fans might have turned their back on the club, they have truly become integral to its rescue and with luck they can look forward to a change in fortune. There has to be a lesson there for us. We have to believe that our support is key to the very survival of our fantastic club and whatever happens I will be there next season. I am already taking a keen and optimistic peek at the National League! Half full? Perhaps – but surely we must always be optimistic and I look forward to beginning the next stage in our history, together with you, next season. I can't wait!"

Couldn't put it better myself – not an arsehole after all!

So I looked down the table, the promotions and the relegations, and found that there were still a few places I hadn't been. In the current division, Morecambe, Notts County and Hartlepool; and I might finally also get to see a game at the Wham Stadium. Of the relegated clubs, I'd been to Doncaster but not Colchester, Blackpool or Crewe. I'd been to both promoted clubs, Grimsby one of my most depressing experiences ever in the late 70s, and I had vowed never to go back. But Cheltenham had been one of my best away weekends and I'd pay it another visit like a shot. I think there were enough to keep me occupied.

I thought of my matchday trips into the city on the M275, and my mind conjured up images of those poor souls driving their wives to go shopping on a Saturday. Truthfully, good or bad, what else would I do on a winter Saturday?

After all, it's Pompey innit?

Acknowledgements

The idea to write about my experiences follwing a lower division football team only came after an incredibly frustrating night at Dagenham and Redbridge. I sent a one page match report to a couple of friends which was riddled with frustration at our public transport causing me to get to the game late, and bemoaning the dreadful quality of the football. It was like a grumpy old man's rant and I hammered it up for emphasis. One of them said that I should write a book about frustrating football awaydays. On the basis that they say that everyone has at least one book in them, I decided that I'd try to make this one mine.

The first five chaoters were written from memory at the end of the 2014/15 season; the chapters which follow were all written contemporaneously, shortly after each game, in the 2015/16 season. This puts in context the fact that I might refer to managers in a chapter from February who were subsequently sacked in March; or make reference in January to Leicester having a chance of winning the Premier League that season; which any self-respecting football fan now knows that they did.

I wanted ths book to differ from many other books detailing for example trips to all 92 football grounds by souls much hardier and more devoted than I will ever be. There are things to observe and report upon in lower league football towns which wouldn't be apparent in Liverpool, Manchester and London and this book was always intended to be more than a factual report on the cost and quality of the burgers and the cost of admission.

There are many people to thank along the way. My long-suffering wife Michelle for one, for her aquiescence in my weekends and nights away at places around the country. My kids, Nicola, Dan and Paddy, who said I'd never finish a book but encouraged me all along to do so. To the family and friends who knowingly allowed themselves to be subjected to scrutiny, and sometimes ridicule, to provide much of the content for the book.

To my cousin Chris, an ex-pat Pompey for living Baltimore, for acting as my proof-reader.

And finally, to the many who unknowingly or unwittingly assisted in providing me with material, my grateful thanks. I hope if you recognise yourselves you won't be offended by what I've written.